SERVICE SIGN MANUAL

U.S. Fish & Wildlife Service

TABLE OF CONTENTS

Chapter 1
Introduction

Chapter 2
Standards

Chapter 3
Procedures

Chapter 4
Sign Maintenance

Chapter 5
Catalog

Appendix 1
Sign Chapter of the Administrative Manual —
3 AM 5 (Draft)

Appendix 2
UNICOR Sign and Decal Products Catalog

Appendix 3
Service Sign and Decal Price List

The U.S. Fish & Wildlife Service would like to thank the U.S.D.A. Forest Service and
the Federal Prison Industries, Inc., for their assistance in producing this publication.

Chapter 1
Introduction

Chapter 1
Introduction

It is the policy of the U.S. Fish and Wildlife Service to provide a uniform system of signs and markers at its stations and centers to inform, guide, educate, and protect its visitors and employees. This manual explains the Service sign program and offers guidance for managing field station sign programs. It is the objective of the Service to bring all signs into conformance with this manual. The development of this manual and the replacement of all signs are part of an effort to:

- Establish uniform standards for Service signs and sign programs nationwide.

- Provide guidelines for planning, ordering, inventorying, installing, inspecting, and maintaining signs.

- Facilitate effective sign program management.

- Provide a catalog of standard Service signs.

- Upgrade all signs to meet legal requirements for reflectivity, readability, and installation.

- Improve the quality and durability of signs.

- Provide a guaranteed system of replacing signs that are defective due to poor manufacturing or quality control.

SIGN PROGRAM GOALS

Goals of the Service sign program include:

- Establishing a uniform appearance and format for signs on all Service lands.

- Establishing visual and verbal consistency for signs within each field station.

- Improving the graphic and aesthetic quality of the signs at each field station.

- Increasing the effectiveness of signs on Service lands, both individually and collectively.

- Reducing accidents and personal injuries on Service lands.

- Reducing costs.

ORGANIZATION OF THIS MANUAL

This manual is organized into the following sections: Introduction, Standards, Procedures, Sign Maintenance, and Catalog of Standard Signs. Appendices include the draft sign chapter of the Administrative Manual, the Federal Prison Industries, Inc. (UNICOR) catalog for standard signs and decals, and the UNICOR price list for Service signs and decals. The latter two Appendices will be updated as prices and product availability change.

STANDARDS

The standards section of the manual provides an overview of Service sign standards. The information in this section of the manual is general in nature and, except as noted, applies to all categories of signs.

PROCEDURES

The procedures section offers guidelines for effective sign program management. Instructions for ordering, inventorying, installing, inspecting, and maintaining signs are provided with illustrative graphics.

SIGN MAINTENANCE

The sign maintenance section provides guidelines and tips for the maintenance and care of all types of signs. Sign repair procedures are also provided. Finally, suggestions for ways to reduce vandalism to signs are offered.

CATALOG

The catalog section is a listing of all standard Service signs. Information is organized by category of sign. Prices of standard signs (signs that can be ordered by order code) are provided in Appendices 2 and 3. Prices of custom signs must be obtained from the vendor.

Signs used on Service lands include:

- Entrance Signs
- U.S. Fee Area Signs
- Area Management Signs
- Information Signs
- Guide Signs
- Interpretive Signs
- The Service Emblem and other Decals
- Federal Recreation Symbol Signs
- Traffic Control Signs and Devices
- Safety Signs

The Catalog section of the manual features **READY REFERENCE GUIDES** for Area Management, Information, and Guide Signs. Ready Reference Guides provide a brief overview of the standards and procedures for these signs. They are intended to be used for quick reference by individuals who are familiar with the Service sign program. They are not intended to replace a thorough reading of the material for those who are new to the Service or unfamiliar with the sign program.

For Traffic Control Signs and devices, Federal Recreation Symbol Signs, Safety Signs, and the Service Emblem and other decals, brief descriptive information is provided along with ordering instructions.

LEGAL REQUIREMENTS FOR SIGN PROGRAMS

Highway Safety Program Standard 13, which appears on page 1-5 of this manual, requires federal agencies with jurisdiction over roadways open to public travel to comply with two standards:

- They must have programs for applying traffic engineering measures and techniques, including the use of signs and other traffic control devices, to reduce the number and severity of traffic accidents on these roads.

- They must evaluate their programs periodically and provide a summary to the Federal Highway Administration.

In fulfillment of these requirements, the U.S. Fish and Wildlife Service sign program includes:

- A sign manual that contains both a catalog of Service signs and guidelines for effective sign program management.

- An inventory system for all signs posted on Service lands (except Area Management, Safety, and Interpretive signs, which are exempt from Standard 13).

- A system for regular sign inspections.

- A program of regular sign maintenance.

- Periodic evaluation of the sign program and appropriate revision of the sign manual.

Other legal authorities regulating the procurement, installation, maintenance, uniformity, and inventory of

Highway Safety Program Standard 13[1]

Traffic Engineering Services

Purpose

To ensure the full and proper application of modern traffic engineering principles and uniform standards for traffic control to reduce the likelihood and severity of traffic accidents.

Standard

Each State, in cooperation with its political subdivisions, and each Federal department or agency which controls highways open to public travel or supervises traffic operations, shall have a program for applying traffic engineering measures and techniques, including the use of traffic control devices, to reduce the number and severity of traffic accidents.

I. The program as a minimum shall consist of:

A. A comprehensive manpower development plan to provide the necessary traffic engineering capability, including:

    1. Provisions for supplying traffic engineering assistance to those jurisdictions unable to justify a full-time traffic engineering staff.

    2. Provisions for upgrading the skills of practicing traffic engineers, and providing basic instruction in traffic engineering techniques to subprofessionals and technicians.

B. Utilization of traffic engineering principles and expertise in the planning, design, construction, and maintenance of the public roadways, and in the application of traffic control devices.

C. A traffic control devices plan including:

    1. An inventory of all traffic control devices.

    2. Periodic review of existing traffic control devices, including a systematic upgrading of substandards issued or endorsed by the Federal Highway Administrator.

    3. A maintenance schedule adequate to ensure proper operation and timely repair of control devices, including daytime and nighttime inspections.

    4. Where appropriate, the application and evaluation of new ideas and concepts in applying control devices to improve their effectiveness through controlled experimentation.

D. An implementation schedule to utilize traffic engineering manpower to:

    1. Review road projects during the planning, designing, and construction stages to detect and correct features that may lead to operational safety difficulties.

    2. Install safety-related improvements as a part of routine maintenance and/or repair activities.

    3. Correct conditions noted during routine operational surveillance of the roadway system to rapidly adjust for the changes in traffic and road characteristics as a means of reducing accident frequency or severity.

    4. Conduct traffic engineering analyses of all high accident locations and develop corrective measures.

    5. Analyze potentially hazardous locations, such as sharp curves, steep grades, and railroad grade crossings and develop appropriate counter-measures.

    6. Identify traffic control needs and determine short- and long-range requirements.

    7. Evaluate the effectiveness of specific traffic control measures in reducing the frequency and severity of traffic accidents.

    8. Conduct traffic engineering studies to establish traffic regulations such as fixed or variable speed limits.

II. This program shall be periodically evaluated by the State, or appropriate Federal department or agency where applicable, and the Federal Highway Administration shall be provided with an evaluation summary.

1. Administered by the Federal Highway Administration

Service signs are summarized in 3 AM 5.4 of the Administrative Manual for the Fish and Wildlife Service. 3 AM 5 appears in Appendix 1 of this manual.

FIELD STATION RESPONSIBILITIES

Field station managers must ensure that stations under their management meet the legal requirements regarding signs. These requirements are summarized below and described in more detail in relevant sections of this manual. *Field station managers can be held personally liable for accidents that result from improper use or care of signs on stations under their jurisdiction.*

INVENTORY

Each field station must maintain a current written inventory of all signs used on refuges, especially signs that are needed to satisfy Title 13. (Area Management, Safety, and Interpretive Signs are exempt from this requirement). This inventory will serve as the backbone of the sign program. These inventory needs can be met by careful use of the Service Custom Sign Order Form (3-2040). Information on completing this form can be found in the Procedures Section of this manual. The new order form integrates the inventorying procedure into the ordering process; therefore, when replacement signs are ordered and installed, using the new order form will update ordering and installation records to meet legal requirements. This form is an integral part of individual field station sign plans (See page 3-14).

Because of Title 13 considerations (tort claims), field stations should be prepared to provide information from their sign inventories to the Regional and Washington Offices if requested to do so. A separate listing of signs needed to satisfy highway safety requirements must also be maintained.

MOUNTING AND INSTALLATION

Each field station must ensure that all signs on the station are properly installed. Proper installation includes location, placement, and mounting.

INSPECTION

Each field station must conduct an annual maintenance inspection of all signs in its inventory of existing public-use road signs and complete a sign maintenance inspection form. Instructions for conducting inspections are provided in the procedures section of this manual. The sign inspection forms are held at the field station and used, if needed, to document compliance with legal and Service requirements.

MAINTENANCE

Each field station must perform all maintenance necessary to ensure that its signs fulfill their purposes and convey a positive image of the Service.

REGIONAL OFFICE RESPONSIBILITIES

Each Regional Office is responsible for overseeing the sign program for the Region. Each Region shall appoint a Regional coordinator/representative to the Service Sign Committee. Specific functions of the Regional Sign Coordinators are listed in 3 AM 5.5E of the Service Administrative Manual. (See Appendix 1).

Other Regional Office responsibilities include periodic review of field station sign programs and inventories and necessary revisions to these inventories, review of all custom design sign orders, and providing assistance in the planning and design of Interpretive Signs. Other Regional personnel such as graphics illustrators, outdoor recreation planners, landscape architects, interpretive specialists, and engineers may be requested to assist in meeting signing objectives.

Chapter 2
Standards

Chapter 2
Standards

SIGN SELECTION

Selection of Sign Type

In general, signs on Service lands are selected according to their functions. The following information can be used as general guidelines to select the type of sign needed.

Entrance Signs

These signs identify field stations by name and identify the Service as the managing agency.

Area Management Signs

Boundary Signs – These signs are placed at regular intervals to mark the boundaries of Service lands. There are four different types of boundary signs: U.S. Fish and Wildlife Service, National Wildlife Refuge, Waterfowl Production Area, and Conservation Easement Signs.

Designated Area Signs – These signs facilitate the management of Service lands by identifying special areas or functions of specific areas and by describing permitted and prohibited activities within designated areas.

Information Signs

General Information Signs – These signs inform visitors of services, opportunities, and entrance or user fees at a field station.

Building Designation Signs – These signs identify specific buildings and, if appropriate, show their hours of operation.

Concession Area Signs – These signs identify concession operations and provide information on rates or fees for commercial goods or services offered.

U.S. Fee Area Signs – These signs identify areas that have entrance fees and/or user fees, and are posted at each designated unit and other appropriate locations.

Guide Signs

General Guide Signs – These signs tell visitors how to find things on Service lands.

Advance Notice Signs – These signs are placed off Service lands to direct visitors to destinations on Service lands. They generally include information about visiting hours or seasons and fees, if applicable.

Interpretive Signs

These signs provide educational information. They usually answer visitors' basic questions and point out or describe a field station's key resources and issues. Interpretive Signs may include trail markers, interior exhibit panels, or exterior exhibit and orientation panels, to name a few.

Traffic Control Devices

Traffic control devices include all signs, signals, markings, and devices placed on, over, or adjacent to roads to regulate, warn, or guide traffic. The selection, design, and placement of these signs and of any other signs intended to be read from public-use roads is governed by guidelines and regulations set forth in the *Manual on Uniform Traffic Control Devices (MUTCD)*.

Federal Recreation Symbols

These symbols graphically inform visitors of available services and of permitted and prohibited activities on Service lands. They may be used alone, on guide signs, and on information and interpretive signs.

Safety Signs

Safety Instruction Signs – These signs provide general information and rules relating to health, first aid, and safety.

Caution Signs – These signs call attention to potential dangers or hazards.

Danger Signs – These signs indicate immediate and grave danger, and prohibit activities risking such dangers.

Hazard Signs – These signs identify dangerous or potentially dangerous materials and the places where they are stored.

Notice Signs – These signs provide information defining and controlling access or circulation.

Safety Equipment/Directions Signs – These signs label or direct viewers to fire extinguishing equipment, fire escapes and exits, gas shut-off valves, and sprinkler drains. They also list safety procedures.

Service Emblem

This emblem is the identifying symbol of the U.S. Fish and Wildlife Service. It can be made of different materials and is used on Entrance Signs, many area signs, and most Service vehicles (except law enforcement vehicles used for undercover work).

FOR OFFICIAL USE ONLY
U.S. GOVERNMENT

Decals

Along with the Service emblem decal, other decals are used to identify the Service or Service objectives by placement on official vehicles, equipment, and exhibits.

Selection Of Sign Materials

Factors to consider in selecting materials for signs include durability, initial cost, maintenance, ease of repair, legibility, night-time visibility, and aesthetics. The materials described below offer the best combination of these attributes, and are therefore the standard.

Substrate

High-density-only (HDO) plywood is the standard for most Service signs. This material is specified because it is durable, requires minimal maintenance, and because reflective sheeting can be applied to meet requirements for night-time visibility. The use of alternate substrates will be authorized only under special circumstances. Should HDO plywood not meet a station's needs, the Regional Sign Coordinator should be contacted for guidance.

Sign Face

Reflective sheeting used on a plywood substrate is durable, requires minimal maintenance, and provides the legally required night-time visibility. Reflective sheeting on plywood is guaranteed for 5 years, and will generally last longer.

Exceptions

The following classes of signs may be exempted from the above material standards:

- **Entrance Signs** – These signs may be manufactured using either HDO plywood or cedar, redwood, or other suitable dimensional lumber. If dimensional lumber is used, the sign face will be either routed or sandblasted.

- **Area Management Signs** – Because of the large number of area management signs ordered, these signs are aluminum with a painted non-reflective surface to take advantage of lower production costs. Aluminum signs are also easier to carry in the field and less expensive to ship in bulk.

DESIGN STANDARDS FOR SERVICE SIGNS

Overview

This section describes the principles of sign design. It includes information on message preparation and legend content as well as panel design. Since national uniformity is a goal of the Service sign program, there is limited opportunity for design variations in signs or symbols. However, an understanding of design principles is helpful in making decisions about the selection and use of signs as well as in facilitating overall management of a station sign program.

A uniform system of attractive, well-maintained signs enhances the Service's identity and image and promotes public recognition of Service goals and objectives. In addition, it provides a finished look to Service field stations and assists visitors in identifying sign messages.

MUTCD Design Requirements

Federal law requires that signs intended for viewing from roads open to the public meet the design standards set forth in the MUTCD. Most Service signs are designed to meet these standards. MUTCD design standards are expressed in terms of the following basic considerations:

- Features such as size, contrast, colors, shape, composition, and reflectorization should combine to draw attention to the sign.

- Shape, size, colors, and simplicity of message should combine to produce a clear meaning.

- Legibility and size should combine with placement to permit adequate time for response.

- Uniformity, size, legibility, and message should combine to command respect.

Specific elements of sign design are presented in the sections that follow. The first section discusses sign messages. It includes information on message information and legend content. The second section discusses panel design. It includes information on typography, color, layout, and size.

Message

A sign is designed for the first-time viewer. It is important that sign messages be brief and easy to understand. These guidelines apply to sign messages:

- Messages should be brief. Messages on all signs except interpretive signs should be four words or fewer, unless the message includes a destination or area name that is longer.

- Messages should contain only essential information. Unnecessary information causes confusion.

- Most signs should express a single thought in a single message. Some Guide Signs and some Information Signs may need to convey more than one message, but a single sign should not have more than four messages.

- The language used in sign messages should be simple and consistent. The words chosen should be words visitors will be familiar and comfortable with. Station areas, offices, and features should be labeled and referred to in a consistent manner.

- Sign messages should present information in a logical order. The most important information should appear on the first line.

- The message should be stated with wording that is positive unless it reduces the clarity of the idea. As a rule-of-thumb, ninety percent of a station's signs should have a positive tone.

- Messages should use commonly recognized abbreviations, such as:

Mount(ain)= Mt	River = R
Saint = St	Bridge = Br
Highway = Hwy	Point = Pt
Road = Rd	Feet = Ft
Lake = Lk	Yards = Yds
Pond = Pd	Mile(s) = Mi
Brook = Bk	Visitor Center = VC

- Signs will not have periods after the above abbreviations.

- Only standard symbols from approved lists may be used in sign messages. For Safety Signs, OSHA standard symbols are used. On all other signs, Federal Recreation symbols may be used.

Typography

Helvetica medium letter style is used on all Service signs (except the Entrance Sign) with lettering options. Both upper and lower case letters should be used, except in acronyms.

Letter size is selected so the sign will be readable from the viewing distance desired. Generally, the lettering on signs that will be read from moving vehicles will be larger than the lettering on signs that will be read by pedestrians. Letter size on Information and Guide Signs is determined by the sign manufacturer according to the viewing distance and/or vehicle speed specified on the Service Custom Sign Order Form (3-2040). Few other instances require letter-size information from station managers.

ABC
abcd

When placing orders for these signs, bear in mind that larger letter sizes may necessitate larger signs. The order form allows the person placing the order to have the manufacturer either fabricate the sign according to specified dimensions or to determine the sign size according to the requested layout. If questions arise, the Regional Sign Coordinator should be consulted.

Color

Color is predetermined for most Service signs. The only Service signs with color options are Interpretive Signs, which may be any color. The following considerations affect color choices for signs:

- Color association – Many sign types inherit their color standards from other sign color systems. These include the MUTCD for traffic control signs and OSHA for safety-related signs. The communicative value of signs is increased if signs with similar functions are consistent in their color combinations.

- **Backgrounds and borders** – Contrast between letter color and background color is necessary for sign legibility, and legibility is increased when a light letter color is used on a dark color background. Borders also improve sign legibility by separating the sign legend from the environment behind the sign. A sign's borders should be the same color as its lettering.

Layout

The layout of information on a sign should combine with letter size to draw attention to the sign and with simplicity of wording to produce a clear message. Guidelines for arranging messages on a sign are:

- Show destinations in the following sequence:

  - straight-ahead arrows, lowest mileage first

  - left-turn arrows, lowest mileage first

  - right-turn arrows, lowest mileage first

  - Place straight-ahead arrows and left-turn arrows at the left margin.

  - Place right-turn arrows at the right margin.

  - Limit messages to four per sign.

  - Make separate signs for permitted and prohibited activities.

Size

Overall sign size is usually determined by the manufacturer. However, there are two occasions when a particular size sign may be requested by the field station:

1. When the space a sign must fit into is limited, the particular size may be requested.

2. When the sign is to be placed under an existing sign, it should be no wider than the other sign.

If necessary, sign size can be calculated from the amount of text and the size of the letters, using the table below. Top, bottom, and side margins should be at least the height of a lower case letter. When measuring letter size, only flat letters (abdefhiklmnprtvwxyz) should be used because the round letters (cgjoqsu) will not give an accurate measurement. When calculating the sign size, remember to include spaces.

Letter And Space Calculation Table For Approximate Length Of Legend

Multiply the number of letters used by the measure given to arrive at the length of line.

Helvetica Medium Letters

Upper Case	Lower Case	Multiply By
2" height	1 1/2" height	1 5/8" per letter
2 3/4" height	2" height	2 1/4" per letter
3 1/2"height	2 1/2"height	2 5/8" per letter
4" height	3" height	3 1/8" per letter
5 1/2 height	4" height	4 3/8" per letter
8" height	6" height	6 1/4" per letter
10 1/2"height	8" height	8 5/8" per letter

Wood Routed — Helvetica

Upper Case	Lower Case	Multiply By
1 1/4" height	7/8" height	1 5/8" per letter
2 1/2" height	1 7/8" height	1 3/4" per letter
3 5/8" height	2 3/4" height	2 1/2" per letter
4 3/4" height	3 1/2" height	3 1/2" per letter
6" height	4 7/8" height	5 1/2" per letter
8" height	6" height	7" per letter

Sign Placement

Overview

Correct placement of signs along public use roads is necessary in order to:

- comply with highway safety laws and MUTCD requirements.

- decrease the likelihood or severity of accidents.

- aid in law enforcement.

- facilitate public awareness of regulations, directions, information, facilities, and resources.

- promote aesthetics, uniformity, and a positive image of the Service.

MUTCD Placement Guidelines

All signs intended to be viewed or read from roads used by the public must conform to placement standards set forth in the *Manual on Uniform Traffic Control Devices*. Detailed placement standards for traffic control signs can be found in section 1-A of the MUTCD. Detailed placement standards for all other signs are found in the catalog section of this manual listed by type of sign. Some general placement guidelines taken from those sections are considered here.

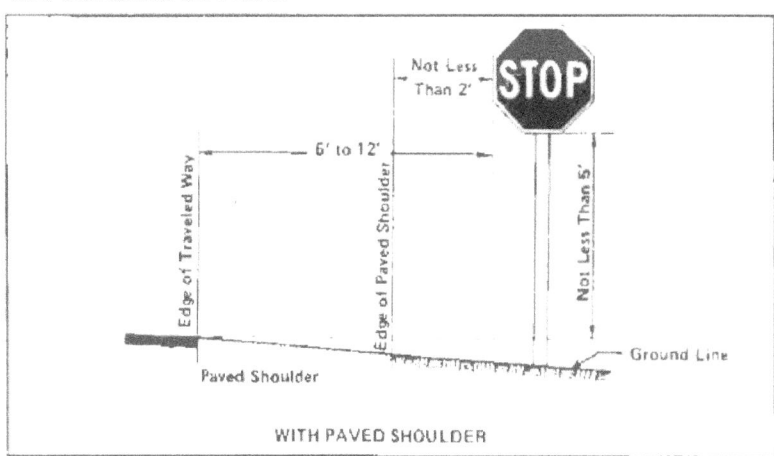

WITH PAVED SHOULDER

Lateral Clearance

Lateral clearance is the horizontal distance between a sign and the edge of the traveled way. The speed of the viewer determines the amount of lateral clearance. For viewers traveling at higher speeds, lateral clearance needs to be greater than for viewers traveling at slower speeds. The relationship between viewer speed and lateral clearance is standardized in the MUTCD. Signs should never be closer than six feet from the edge of a road shoulder, or 12 feet from the traveled portion of a road with no shoulder. Lateral clearance is not a consideration for pedestrian signs.

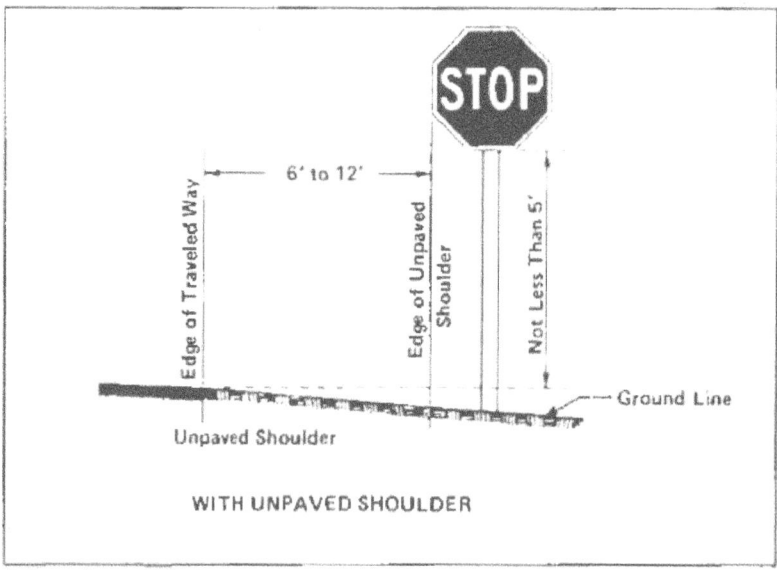

WITH UNPAVED SHOULDER

Viewing Distance

Viewing distance is the distance between the sign and the farthest point from which it is meant to be read. Viewing distance is determined by traffic speed; the higher the speed, the further the sign should be placed from where drivers will need to be able to read it. The relationship between traffic speed and viewing distance is standardized:

- At 25 mph., eye focus is at 600 feet ahead of car.

- At 45 mph., eye focus is at 1,200 feet ahead of car.

- At 60 mph., eye focus is at 1,400 feet ahead of car.

Viewing distance is only a minor consideration for pedestrian signs.

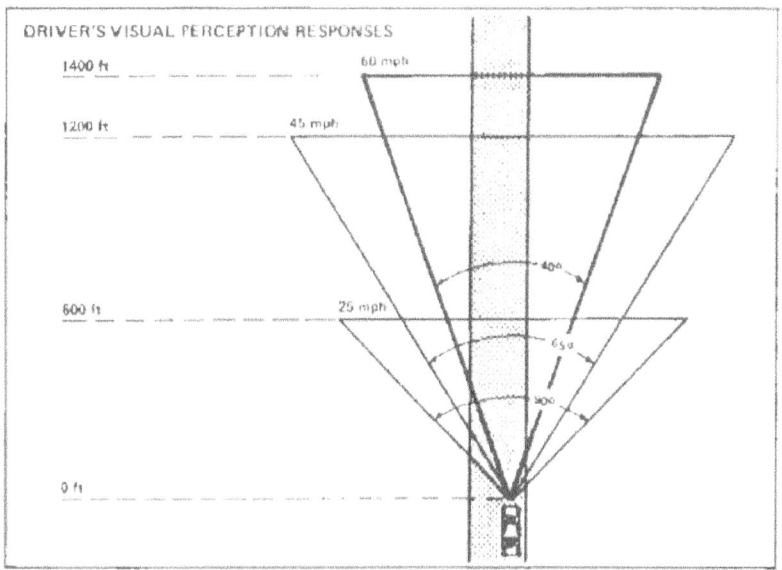

Position

Signs must be placed within the driver's immediate field of vision. Drivers cannot be expected to turn their heads to read a sign. Signs mounted more than 40 feet off the roadway may require use of a larger panel to increase readability because the sign is outside the normal field of vision.

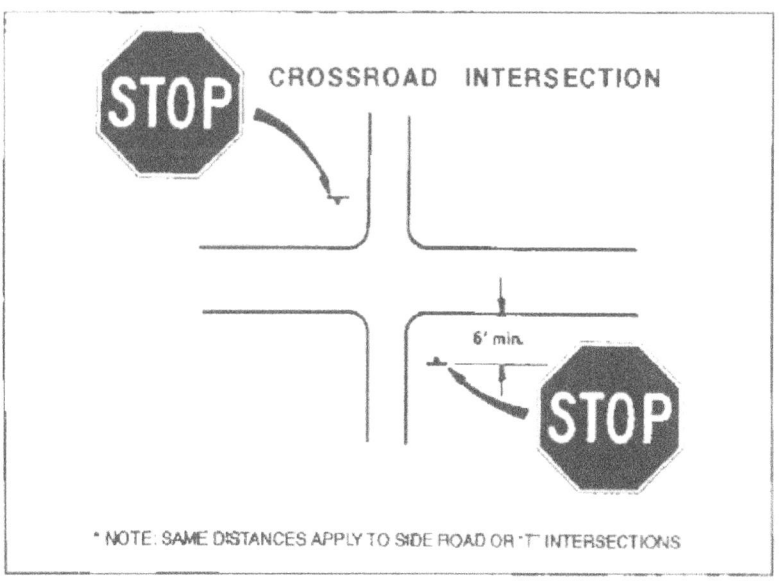

Signs must be placed on the right side of the roadway wherever possible. A driver is not conditioned to look to the left side of the road for critical driving information. Exceptions include:

- signs on the left shoulder of a road where these are directly in front of approaching vehicles, as on sharp curves to the right.

- a two-sided entrance sign to a field station that is placed on one side of the road.

Siting

Signs placed along roads must be placed in such a location that they can be mounted on bases, posts, or poles and conform with other placement guidelines. **Signs closer than 30 feet to the road must be mounted on breakaway supports unless they are protected by guardrails or topographic change. (See page 3-22).** Because of grade differences or other obstructions, it may be necessary to regrade a site, clear or relocate obstructions, or have a traffic engineering study performed.

Signs meant to be viewed by pedestrians shall be placed on bases, posts, poles, fences, or buildings, as applicable. Signs should not be placed on trees.

All signs should be sited where they are easily noticed but do not interfere with and are not obscured by the natural growth and physical features of an area. In addition, all potential obstructions to visibility, such as tree limbs that could press down in front of a sign face under the weight of heavy snow, should be anticipated.

Spacing

Signs visible from the road should be placed and spaced in a uniform manner throughout a field station in accordance with MUTCD guidelines. Generally, signs placed on public-use roads should be at least 100 feet apart to give drivers enough time to read and react safely to one sign before another is presented.

Safety

Signs should be placed so that they are not distractions or hazards. They should be located to maximize legibility, minimize the effects of mud splatter, and conform with safety guidelines related to fixed obstacles near roads. Signs should not obscure each other and should not be hidden from view by other roadside objects.

Proper authorities should be consulted before digging post holes to ensure that posts will not interfere with underground utilities, drainage structures, other underground equipment, and cultural resources.

Angle

Sign faces should always be perpendicular to the approaching viewer. Signs should never be placed parallel to passing traffic. If reflection from the sign face impairs legibility, the sign should be turned slightly away from the road. Signs located 30 feet or more from the pavement edge should be turned toward the road. On curves, the angle of the sign should be determined by the course of approaching traffic. Sign faces are normally vertical; however, the faces of all overhead signs should be tilted at least 3 degrees downward towards traffic. This will help to ensure that dirt, dust, snow, and bird droppings do not fall onto the sign face. Sign faces may also be tilted forward or backward from the vertical position to improve the viewing angle on grades.

Height

Heights for MUTCD signs along roads are standardized; the lower edges of primary signs must be a minimum of 5 feet above the road level. A lower grade next to a roadway should be raised prior to mounting a sign.

Normally signs to be read by pedestrians should be placed at 5'5", unless this would create an obstruction, as with an interpretive sign blocking the view of its subject. Larger signs posted in large spaces or for viewing at greater distances can be placed proportionally higher. Generally, all letters, words, and symbols on a sign should fall within a 10 degree visual cone for the reader (roughly proportionately equivalent to the width of the hand held at arm's length). When placing signs, remember that some of the readers will be disabled (e.g., in wheelchairs), and that consideration needs to be given so that signs are at an appropriate height and/or of an appropriate size to accommodate these people.

Field Test

A good way to verify the appropriateness of a sign's placement is to place a piece of cardboard or brown paper, the same size as the proposed sign, in the proposed location. For signs viewed from a moving vehicle, testing will include driving the approach from which the sign is to be viewed.

Planning

A station sign program must carefully consider the relationship a given sign has to others and to the overall station operation. A Sign Plan provides a vehicle for this consideration while documenting sign history and purpose, and providing for review by the Regional sign coordinator and line supervisor.

The format for a Sign Plan should be simple, containing the custom sign order forms, a vicinity map, maintenance schedules, and a review and approval page.

Maps should be as simple as possible while still clearly documenting placement of individual signs. Small stations can probably use a single, letter-size station map to locate and number all signs. Large stations can use a system of nested maps showing the location of an enlarged view on the first map by an A, B, etc., with map A being a small scale view of the intersection or area showing the location of signs A-1", A-2", etc. The maps are where sign numbers are assigned and are important for recordkeeping functions, including the inventory.

The plan should be submitted to the Regional Sign Coordinator and line supervisor for review. The station keeps the original sign plan after approval, and the Regional Sign Coordinator keeps a copy.

Amendments to the plan are necessary to keep the plan up to date. When a new sign is needed, a new custom sign order form and map should be submitted to the Regional Sign Coordinator and line supervisor for approval, and attached to all copies of the plan.

Chapter 3
Procedures

Chapter 3
Procedures

ORDERING SIGNS

Sign ordering procedures and sources are standardized. This simplifies the ordering process, promotes greater uniformity in signs at all field stations, and reduces costs.

Field stations are not permitted to make signs. Under 18 USC 4124, most standard signs (Area management, Information, Guide, Traffic Control, Federal Recreation Symbol Signs, and Safety Signs, and the Service Emblem and other decals) must be ordered from Federal Prison Industries, Inc. (UNICOR).

Ordering Standard Signs

Standard signs with no options, including Area Management Signs, Traffic Control Signs, Federal Recreation Symbol Signs, and Service Emblems and Decals, can be ordered through UNICOR by order code number on a Purchase Order (3-2103). Current prices are listed for all standard signs in Appendices 2 and 3 of this manual. The Purchase Order should normally be submitted to the Regional Sign Coordinator for approval; however, Regional Sign Coordinators may, at their discretion, waive the requirement for Regional approval and authorize field station managers to order these types of signs by submitting the Purchase Order directly to UNICOR.

Occasionally, the Washington Office requests consolidation of orders for standard signs at the Regional level. Although this procedure is time-consuming, it can reduce administrative costs substantially.

Under emergency situations, signs may be procured from private sources. At the earliest opportunity, these signs will be replaced by approved standard signs whenever possible.

Ordering Custom Signs

General

Entrance Signs, Information Signs, Guide Signs, and Federal Recreation Symbol Signs with arrows or text must be ordered with the Custom Sign Order Form (FWS-3-2040). This form can be obtained from the Regional Sign Coordinator or photocopied from Exhibit 1 on page 3-14 of this manual. A separate form must be completed for each type of sign needed. Any sign ordered using the Custom Sign Order Form must be accompanied by an Acquisition Request (FWS-3-2109) or Purchase Order (3-2103).

The Custom Sign Order forms should be submitted to the Regional Sign Coordinator, who will validate the order, amend it if necessary, and notify the station placing the order if a change is needed.

Orders for custom Guide, Information, and Federal Recreation Symbol Signs are placed with UNICOR using a Purchase Order (3-2103). A price estimate can be obtained from the Regional Sign Coordinator by telephone prior to submission of the Custom Sign Order and Purchase Order forms for review. In some instances, an order can be submitted as not to exceed, with UNICOR providing exact cost information at time of delivery. A copy of the approved order will be returned to the ordering station.

Orders for Interpretive and other one-of-a-kind signs may be placed with the Winona Sign Center or other contractually approved sources using an Acquisition Request (3-2109). The Regional Sign Coordinator can provide price estimates. The Acquisition Request and Custom Sign Order Form are submitted to the Regional Sign Coordinator for review and processing. A copy of the approved order will be returned to the ordering station.

Orders for Entrance Signs will be placed on an Acquisition Request and submitted along with the Custom Sign Order Form to the Regional Sign Coordinator for review and approval. The approved order will be forwarded to CGS for processing with the appropriate vendor. A copy of the approved and obligated order will be returned to the ordering station.

When the signs ordered have been received and accepted by the station as meeting all Service requirements, the vendor's invoice should be approved and processed promptly, in accordance with the Prompt Payment Act.

Any signs received by field stations that do not conform to the ordering requirements must be returned to the vendor immediately with a letter explaining the deficiency(ies). A copy of the letter must be forwarded to the Regional Sign Coordinator, who will, in turn, forward it to the National Sign Coordinator. UNICOR has requested that a telephone contact be made prior to making returns.

The Custom Sign Order Form
The following information pertains to filling out the Custom Sign Order Form:

- Sections I and II. Self Explanatory.

- Section III. The standard substrate for information and guide signs is 3/4" High Density Overlay plywood. The HDO plywood has proven to be superior to aluminum and most other substrates through extensive field testing.

These signs will be produced with square corners (except Entrance Signs which have 3" radius corners) which will be lightly bevelled. The edges of the signs will be sealed and painted brown to match the brown reflective sheeting which will be affixed to the face of the signs. White reflective, helvetica medium letters will be used (optima medium on the entrance signs), and the message will be in both upper and lower case letters. Complete specifications for the standard Service Entrance Sign are available through Regional Sign Coordinators.

A narrow strip of white reflective border tape will be affixed to the front edge of the signs. The border tape will have radius corners and give the illusion that the signs are cut with radius corners. Brown reflective tape will be used on bicolor signs to highlight the white background.

- Section IV. Letter sizes selected for a sign are determined by vehicle speed and/or viewing distance according to the standards in the Manual on Uniform Traffic Control Devices (MUTCD). The letter sizes displayed on the Custom Sign Order Form (10 1/2", 8", 5 1/2", and 4") represent the upper case letters. The accompanying lower case letters will be proportionately smaller. If more than one letter size is selected for a single sign, the smaller letter sizes should meet MUTCD standards, especially for vehicle traffic signs.

- Section V. Self explanatory.

- Section VI. Include marginal notes and comments as appropriate to ensure that the sign drawing will be interpreted correctly by the Regional Sign Coordinator and sign vendor.

- Sections VII — IX. Self explanatory.

- Section X. The Other Requesting Signature Approval will generally be the next-in-line regional supervisor.

Sign Warranties

All signs purchased from UNICOR and the Winona Sign Shop are warranted to be free of manufacturer's defects for a period of five (5) years from original date of receipt (not installation). This includes delamination of facing materials, loss of reflectivity, legibility, severe fading or premature weathering. Vandalism and wind sand blasting are not covered. To file a warranty claim, return the failed sign to UNICOR along with proof of original delivery date and, if possible, the original work order number. This information should be gathered as a matter of routine and kept in the station sign files.

Vinyl sheeting and reflective sheeting signs purchased from the Winona Sign Shop are warranted for seven (7) years from date of receipt. Routed and sandblasted signs from the above sources are not warranted other than to be manufactured to specifications. Similar procedures are followed as above to claim warranty adjustments.

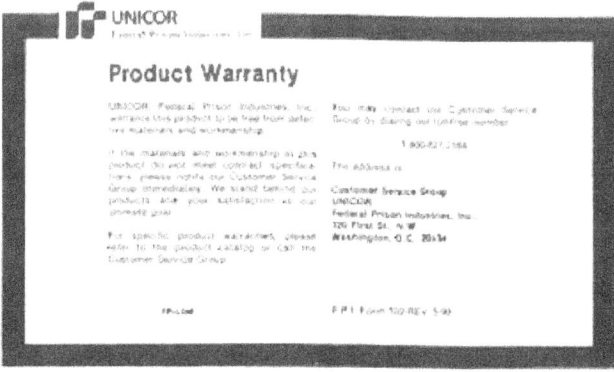

MOUNTING AND INSTALLATION

Standard Mounting Methods

Standardized sign mounting methods are used for most signs except Entrance signs and Interpretive signs to create visual uniformity on Service facilities. (Two sided signs may be used. There are various ways to mount them. Regional Sign Coordinators should be consulted for advice).

There are three main ways to mount signs:

- **Ground mounting** — Mounting a sign on a foundation or base that is level with the ground. These foundations may be concrete, brick, or wood.

- **Post mounting** — Mounting a sign on a post or posts fixed in the ground. Posts may be wood, metal, or other materials (e.g. Carsonite), although wood posts are preferable in most instances (see additional information on post mounting below).

- **Wall mounting** — Mounting a sign on a vertical surface such as a building wall or door.

The mounting method should be appropriate for the type of sign and the viewing requirements. Area management Signs, Guide Signs, Traffic Control Signs, and Federal Recreation Symbols are usually mounted on posts. Building Designation Signs, Safety Signs, and interpretive panels are often wall mounted. Information Signs may be either post or wall mounted.

Post-mounted signs should be mounted on wood posts in most cases. Wooden signposts used consistently throughout a facility are visually more harmonious with the surrounding landscape and provide a more finished look than metal posts. A 4 x 4" or 4" x 6" chromated copper arsenate (CCA) treated wood post, number 2 or better, that is well seasoned and free of defects is the standard post for most signs. The use of metal or synthetic (e.g. Carsonite) posts is acceptable in these instances:

- For posting signs in remote areas away from general public view; for example, boundary signs in remote areas.

- When replacing a sign mounted on a metal post that is still in good condition.

- When the use of a flexible post may be a safety consideration (e.g. in a parking area where the post may be struck by vehicles).

Exhibit 5 on page 3-21 illustrates determining how many posts are needed to support sign panels of varying sizes. Signs up to 36 inches across can be placed on a single post, signs 37 to 72 inches across should be mounted on two posts, and signs 73 to 96 inches across should be mounted on three posts.

Signs posted within 30 feet of a road where the speed limit is 35 mph or more should be installed on yielding or breakaway posts unless they are protected by guardrails or topographic change. This applies even if the sign is not intended to be read from the road. The following criteria apply to wood posts:

- Single wood posts that are less than 24 square inches in cross section (6" x 4" or smaller) need no breakaway treatment.

- Two posts, each with a cross section no larger than 3" X 6" or 4" X 5" need no breakaway treatment.

- Three posts, each with a cross section no larger than 3" X 5" or 4" X 4" need no breakaway treatment.

- Larger wood posts can be made to break away by drilling 3 holes through the post starting 4 to 6 inches above the ground and spaced every 6 inches. The diameter of the hole should be 1/3 the thickness of the post. This does not result in significant loss of wind loading capacity or structural strength. Holes should be treated with CCA preservative. Breakaway notches may also be used. Exhibit 6 on page 3-22 gives examples of suitable breakaway designs for wooden sign supports. The U.S. Department of Transportation has further information on various breakaway designs developed by state and federal agencies for sign applications.

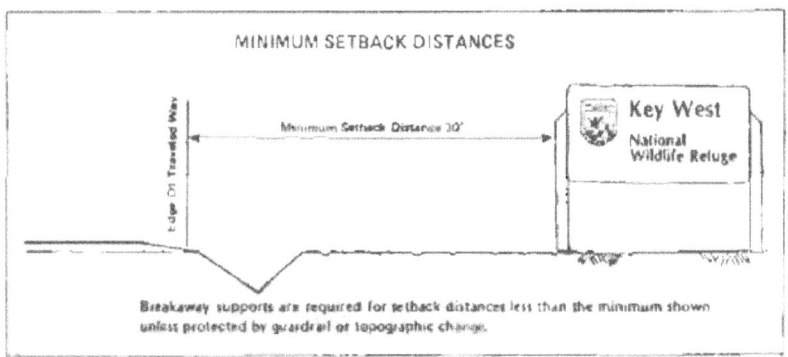

Guidelines for Installing Signs

- Signs should be positioned so there is a clear line of sight from the viewing point to the sign face.

- Sign supports and their foundations should be constructed to hold signs in the proper position and to resist swaying in the wind or removal by vandals.

- Concrete foundations for signposts or supports should be at or below ground level.

- The lower edges of primary signs should be at least 5 feet above ground level.

- Signs posted on roads where the speed limit is 35 mph or more should be at least 12 feet from the edge of the traveled way.

- Signs posted within 30 feet of a road where the speed limit is 35 mph or more should be mounted on breakaway posts unless they are protected by a guardrail or topographic change.

- Anti-theft, anti-vandal fasteners and hardware should be used to mount signs. The Vandlgard nut assembly (shown in Exhibit 7), which includes the nut, bolt, and nylon washer, can be purchased from UNICOR.

INVENTORY AND INSPECTION

Sign Inventory

The sign inventory is a system of recording the place and date of installation and documenting compliance with manufacturing requirements for certain types of signs. Sign inventories must be kept to meet Highway Safety Standard 13 legal requirements for Traffic Control signs and devices and for signs placed along public-access roads, such as Information Signs, Guide Signs, and some Federal Recreation Symbol Signs.

Highway Safety Standard 13 states that a record must be kept of when and where signs are installed and that documentation must be available to confirm compliance with readability and reflectivity requirements. This documentation is not required for Area Management, Safety, and Interpretive Signs or signs along auto tour routes, because these signs are read by pedestrians or slow moving vehicles and therefore are not subject to Highway Safety Standard 13.

The new ordering procedures eliminate the need to separately inventory signs by incorporating inventorying into the new Custom Sign Order Form (FWS-3-2040). Properly completed, this form provides all the information and documentation necessary for the inventory of these types of signs. Even though Traffic Control Signs and devices and Federal Recreation Symbol Signs are not ordered using the FWS-3-2040 form, the form still must be completed and attached to a copy of the purchase order and filed in a separate inventory file when these signs are installed. This ensures proper documentation of the installation date and place and will support tort claim liabilities. When the signs are ordered from the authorized source (UNICOR), the reflectivity and readability are ensured via specifications provided to the manufacturer.

Proper completion of the FWS-3-2040 form also provides the documentation and information necessary to enforce guarantees and obtain replacements for signs that fail due to poor manufacturing practices or poor quality control. A separate file for signs will facilitate retrieval of this information.

Exhibits 2, 3 and 4 are samples of properly completed sign order forms.

Sign Inspection

Legal Requirements

Regular inspection of all traffic signs — all signs posted for viewing from roads open to the public — is a legal requirement under Highway Safety Standard Program 13, which appears on page 1-5 of this manual. All of these signs should be inspected annually. In addition, regular (biannual) inspection of all other signs on Service lands is an integral part of good sign program management. At the field station, inspections provide information for maintenance plans; at the national and Regional levels, they provide useful information for sign ordering and future budget estimates and justifications.

The Service standard for traffic sign inspection is a complete on-site review (including day and nighttime inspections) of all signs on public-use roads, conducted annually. These signs must appear on each station's current inventory of existing signs.

Including all station signs in these inspections is recommended to ensure that they are still needed and are properly maintained. This is regarded as sound, cost-effective management, but it is not a legal requirement.

General Considerations for Sign Inspection

Sign inspections should be conducted by a staff member familiar with sign maintenance procedures and legal requirements. However, all employees should be observant of sign conditions and report damaged or obscured signs immediately. A sign inspection includes these considerations:

- Is the sign in place?

- Is the sign properly installed?

- Is the sign still necessary?

- Is the sign upright and facing in the right direction?

- Is the sign easily seen (i.e. unobscured by vegetation, structures, etc.)?

- Are the sign's support structure or foundation in good condition?

- Is the face in good condition?

- Is the sign's reflectivity still effective?

- Is the surface clean?

- Does the sign comply with the standards of this manual?

Inspecting the Sign

The following guidelines should be used for inspecting each part of a sign:

- **Substrate** — Check the substrate for cracks, ply separation, warps, holes, or other damage. The substrate should be level and firmly attached to the supports and base.

- **Face** — If the sign has vinyl or reflective sheeting, check to be sure that it is securely bonded to the panel and free of cracks, tears, scratches, blisters, or other damage. If the sign face is painted, check the surface for cracking, peeling, or blistering.

- **Sign Supports** — Check all supports to ensure that they are firmly placed, plumb, and free from rot, cracks, and holes. Masonry structures should be in a good state of repair, free of cracks and loose mortar. Concrete footings or foundations must be flush with the ground.

- **Braces** — Check all braces to ensure that they are firmly in place and free from cracks or other damage.

- **Hardware** — Check all bolts, nuts, washers, and other fasteners to ensure that they are securely fastened and free from corrosion or other defects.

Inspecting for Nighttime Reflectivity

Studies have shown that while only about a third of vehicle traffic moves after dark, over half of all traffic fatalities occur at night. For this reason, the **Highway Safety Act of 1966 (Standard 13)** requires night inspection of Traffic Control devices. This includes Guide and Information signs intended for viewing from a roadway. Reflective signs should be clearly legible when lit by vehicle headlights on low beam. If not, the sign must be replaced.

Completing the Inspection Form

The Inspection Form is shown in Exhibit 8 on page 3-25; it can be photocopied for field station use. Complete one form for each sign in use and use the form (or one of a similar format) when reviewing signs biannually.

Exhibit 1
U.S. Fish and Wildlife Service
Custom Sign Order Form

FWS-3-2040
Revised 5/87

Section I. Station Information

a. Station Name: _____

b. Shipping Address: _____

_____

c. Organization Code: _____

d. Subactivity No.: _____

e. Phone Number: _____

Section II. Station Ordering Information

a. Purchase Order Number: _____

Acquisition Req. No.: _____

b. Station Sign No.: _____

c. Vendor Code: _____

Unicor (FPI)	1	Other	3
Winona	2	(Describe below)

Section III. Sign type/Substrate/Quantity

a. Type of Sign (Check One)

_____ Entrance Sign

_____ Information Sign

_____ Guide Sign

_____ Interpretive Sign

b. Substrate (Check One)

_____ Sandblasted

_____ Wood-routed

_____ HDO Plywood

_____ HDO Plywood

c. Quantity: _____

_____ Plywood _____ Other (Justify below)

_____ Other (Justify below)

_____ Other (Justify below)

(Attach specifications and drawings)

Section IV. Letter Height Requirements

a. Vehicle Traffic Signs (Check One)

_____ 10½"   50-55 mph   (400 ft. viewing distance)

_____ 8"   50-55 mph (300 ft. viewing distance)

_____ 5½"   35-45 mph (200 ft. viewing distance)

_____ 4"   0-30 mph (75-100 ft. viewing distance)

b. Pedestrian Signs (Check One)

_____ 2¾"   (750100 ft. viewing distance)

_____ 1¼"   (0-75 ft. viewing distance)

_____ 1"   (0-35 ft. viewing distance)

Section V. Layout

Check One Only

_____ Determine sign size according to legend layout and speed of traffic

_____ Fabricate to specified dimensions (Justify below)

Section VI. Sign Message and Rough Drawing

Section VII. Justification

Section VIII. Sign Location	Section IX. Vendor Information	Section X. Signature Block
Description of Location	Price per Sign $ _____ ea. $ _____ ea. $ _____ ea. Vendor Job No _____	Station Manager
Reduced Drawing of Location		Regional Sign Coordinator
Installation Date:	FWS Agency Identification Code 14-16-0006	Other Requesting Signature Approval

INSTRUCTIONS FOR COMPLETING CUSTOM SIGN ORDER FORM

Prepare this form as indicated below and mail a copy of this and the appropriate purchase order/acquisition request to your Regional sign representative. Any orders for signs not on this form, or for hardware or posts (etc. used for installing or maintaining signs) should be ordered via a purchase order with a copy mailed to your Regional Sign Representative.

SPECIFIC INSTRUCTIONS

Section I. Station Information

a.   Station Name. Self-explanatory.

b.   Shipping Address. Enter the complete shipping address, including zip code.

c.   Organization Code. Enter the organization code for your station.

d.   Subactivity Number. Enter the charging cost code component for this procurement.

e.   Phone Number. Enter the phone number for the station, including area code.

Section II. Station Ordering Information

a.   Purchase Order Number. Enter the purchase order number (or the acquisition request number, if appropriate).

b.   Vendor Code Number. Enter the vendor code number. If other, enter the vendor's name.

c.   Station Sign Number. Enter the number the station individually assigns to the sign(s), if applicable

Section III.   Sign Type/Substrate/Quantity

a.   Type of Sign. Check the appropriate box to indicate the type of sign being ordered.

b.   Substrate. Check the appropriate box to indicate the type of substrate (material) you ordered. Please note: The substrate recommended by the Sign committee is the first option listed, all other options must be justified in Section VII. The face and design of the sign is provided in the manufacturing specifications provided to the vendor by the Regional Sign Representative.

c.   Quantity. Enter the number of signs being ordered.

Section IV. Letter Height Requirements

a.   Vehicle Traffic Signs. If the sign is to be viewed by individuals in moving vehicles, check the appropriate letter height requirement based on speed of traffic. The height of the letters indicated in this section is for the upper case letters only.

b.   Pedestrian Signs. If the sign is to be viewed by pedestrians only, check the appropriate letter height based on viewing distance. The height of the letters indicated in this section is for the upper case letters only.

Section V. Layout

a.   Fabricate to specified dimensions. Check this box if the sign must be manufactured to specific dimensions and justify in Section VII.

b.   Determine sign size according to legend layout and speed of traffic. The manufacturer will determine the size of the sign based on your design guidelines provided in Section VI and the letter height requirements indicated in Section IV. This is the preferred method for determining the size of the sign, since legibility is the first consideration.

Section VI. Sign Message and Rough Drawing

Provide a simple sketch of the sign with the appropriate wording and graphics. The letter style, borders, color, and radius are predetermined in the specifications provided by the Regional sign representative.

Section VII. Justification

Enter justification for items requested above or provide any special instructions needed to manufacture the signs(s).

Section VIII. Sign Location

Enter a written description and sketch drawing of where the sign will be installed. If the sign is ordered for inventory purposes and is to be installed at a later date, complete the installation information when the sign is actually installed.

Section IX. Vendor Information

This section is to be completed by the vendor(s). Per vendor codes in Section II, vendor should list price of sign.

Section X. Signature Block

Self-explanatory.

Exhibit 2. Sample Completed Custom Sign Order Form

U.S. Fish and Wildlife Service
Custom Sign Order Form

FWS-3-2040
Revised 5/87

Section I. Station Information

a. Station Name: *National Elk Refuge*   c. Organization Code: *61550*
b. Shipping Address: *675 East Broadway*   d. Subactivity No.: *1261*
   Jackson WY 83001   e. Phone Number: *(307) 733-9212*

Section II. Station Ordering Information

a. Purchase Order Number: *68201-02809*   c. Vendor Code: *1*
   Acquisition Req. No.: _____   Unicor (FPI) 1   Other   3
b. Station Sign No.: *2*   Winona   2   (Describe below)

Section III. Sign type/Substrate/Quantity

a. Type of Sign (Check One)   b. Substrate (Check One)   c. Quantity: *1*

____ Entrance Sign   ____ Sandblasted   ____ Plywood ____ Other (Justify below)
____ Information Sign   ____ Wood-routed   ____ Other (Justify below)
✓ Guide Sign   ____ HDO Plywood   ____ Other (Justify below)
____ Interpretive Sign   ✓ HDO Plywood   (Attach specifications and drawings)

Section IV. Letter Height Requirements

a. Vehicle Traffic Signs (Check One)   b. Pedestrian Signs (Chec...

____ 10½" 50-55 mph (400 ft. viewing distance)   ____ ...ing distance)
____ 8"   50-55 mph (300 ft. viewing distance)   ...distance)
✓   5½"   35-45 mph (200 ft. viewing distance)   ...stance)
____ 4"   0-30 mph   (75-100 ft. viewing distance)

Section V.

Check One Only   ✓ Determine ... layout and speed of traffic
                        ____ Fabricate to ... ...ions (Justify below)

SAMPLE

Section VI. Sign Message and Rough Drawing

Jackson National
Fish Hatchery
1 mile
Open 8am - 4pm

Section VII. Justification	Section IX. Vendor Information	Section X. Signature Block
Section VIII. Sign Location	Price per Sign	Station Manager
Description of Location	$ ____ ea.	*John Ahlrechd*
	$ ____ ea.	Regional Sign Coordinator
	$ ____ ea.	*Maurice Knight*
Reduced Drawing of Location	Vendor Job No ____	Other Requesting Signature Approval
Installation Date: 6-91	FWS Agency Identification Code 14-16-0006	

UNITED STATES
FISH AND WILDLIFE SERVICE
ACQUISITION REQUEST

PAGE 1 OF _____

TO:	REQUESTING OFFICE: TELEPHONE:	REQUISITION/ADVANCED PROCUREMENT PLAN NUMBER.

SUGGESTED VENDORS (NAMES, ADDRESSES)	DELIVER TO:

ITEM OR FORM NO	DETAILED DESCRIPTION	QUANTITY	UNIT	UNIT PRICE	EXTENDED AMOUNT

(PROVIDE ADDITIONAL SHEETS IF NEEDED) | TOTAL ESTIMATED COST | $

1. REQUISITIONED BY (SIGNATURE)	4. PROPERTY CERTIFICATION
	EXCEPT AS NOTED, THE ABOVE ITEMS ARE NOT AVAILABLE FROM ANY GOVERNMENT SOURCE
NAME/TITLE DATE	SIGNATURE
	NAME/TITLE DATE
2. FUND CERTIFICATION	
THE UNDERSIGNED HEREBY CERTIFIES THAT FUNDS IN THE AMOUNT OF $ _____ ARE HEREBY AVAILABLE AND RESERVED FOR THIS TRANSACTION AND AUTHORIZED FOR THE PURPOSE INTENDED.	5. OBJECT CLASS
CHARGED TO:	
SIGNATURE	6. BUREAU/REGIONAL OFFICER (SIGNATURE IF NECESSARY)
NAME/TITLE DATE	NAME/TITLE DATE
3. APPROVED BY (SIGNATURE)	7. BUREAU/REGIONAL OFFICER (SIGNATURE IF NECESSARY)
NAME/TITLE DATE	NAME/TITLE DATE

SIGNATURE BLOCKS 1, 2 AND 3 MUST BE COMPLETED AT THE ORIGINATING OFFICE. BLOCK 2 MUST BE SIGNED BY THE INDIVIDUAL HAVING FISCAL RESPONSIBILITY FOR THE PARTICULAR ACTIVITY. BLOCK 3 MUST BE SIGNED BY THE REQUESTING OFFICE'S PROJECT LEADER/SUPERVISOR OR AT A HIGHER LEVEL AS DETERMINED BY A RESPECTIVE WASHINGTON OR REGIONAL OFFICIAL. BLOCKS 4 AND 5 MUST BE COMPLETED BY THE PROCURING OFFICE. BLOCKS 6 AND 7 ARE OPTIONAL DEPENDING UPON THE PARTICULAR PROCUREMENT.

Exhibit 3. Example of a Completed Acquisition Form

FWS FORM 3-2109
APRIL 1986

UNITED STATES
FISH AND WILDLIFE SERVICE

ACQUISITION REQUEST

PAGE 1 OF _1_

TO: Contracting and General Services	REQUESTING OFFICE: National Elk Refuge. TELEPHONE: (307) 733-9212	REQUISITION/ADVANCED PROCUREMENT PLAN NUMBER: 61550-0029

SUGGESTED VENDORS (NAMES, ADDRESSES):	DELIVER TO:
UNICOR Sign Order Center Data/Graphics Division 320 First St. N.W. Rm #126 Washington, D.C. 20534	National Elk Refuge 675 East Broadway Jackson, WY 83001

ITEM OR FORM NO.	DETAILED DESCRIPTION	QUANTITY	UNIT	UNIT PRICE	EXTENDED AMOUNT
	Standard U.S. Fish and Wildlife Service Area Management Signs (A-series)				
1.	FWS-A-4 (Public Fishing Area)	5	ea	9.95	49.75
2.	FWS-A-5 (Public Hunting Area)	20	ea	7.25	145.00
3	FWS-A-6 (Area Beyond This Sign Closed)	200	ea	5.25	1,050.00

SAMPLE

(PROVIDE ADDITIO... | TOTAL ESTIMATED COST | $ 1,244.75

1. REQUISITIONED BY (SIGNATURE)
NAME/TITLE: James Griffin Asst. Mgn. DATE 3-91

2. FUND CERTIFICATION
THE UNDERSIGNED HEREBY CERTIFIES THAT FUNDS IN THE AMOUNT OF $ 1,244.75 ARE HEREBY AVAILABLE AND RESERVED FOR THIS TRANSACTION AND AUTHORIZED FOR THE PURPOSE INTENDED.
CHARGED TO 61550-1261
SIGNATURE
NAME/TITLE: Same as above DATE 3-91

3. APPROVED BY (SIGNATURE)
NAME/TITLE: John Wilbright Refuge Mgr. DATE 3-91

PROPERTY CERTIFICATION
EXCEPT AS NOTED, THE ABOVE ITEMS ARE NOT AVAILABLE FROM ANY GOVERNMENT SOURCE
SIGNATURE
NAME/TITLE | DATE

5. OBJECT CLASS

6. BUREAU/REGIONAL OFFICER (SIGNATURE IF NECESSARY)
NAME/TITLE | DATE

7. BUREAU/REGIONAL OFFICER (SIGNATURE IF NECESSARY)
NAME/TITLE | DATE

SIGNATURE BLOCKS 1, 2 AND 3 MUST BE COMPLETED AT THE ORIGINATING OFFICE. BLOCK 2 MUST BE SIGNED BY THE INDIVIDUAL HAVING FISCAL RESPONSIBILITY FOR THE PARTICULAR ACTIVITY. BLOCK 3 MUST BE SIGNED BY THE REQUESTING OFFICE'S PROJECT LEADER/SUPERVISOR, OR AT A HIGHER LEVEL AS DETERMINED BY A RESPECTIVE WASHINGTON OR REGIONAL OFFICIAL. BLOCKS 4 AND 5 MUST BE COMPLETED BY THE PROCURING OFFICE. BLOCKS 6 AND 7 ARE OPTIONAL DEPENDING UPON THE PARTICULAR PROCUREMENT.

ORDER FOR SUPPLIES OR SERVICES

Page	of	Pages

IMPORTANT: Mark all packages and papers with contract and/or order numbers.

1. DATE OF ORDER	2. REQUISITIONING OFFICE	3. CONTRACT NO. (if any)	4. ORDER NO.

5. SHIP TO: (Consignee and address, ZIP code)

6. MAIL INVOICE IN TRIPLICATE TO: (Include ZIP code) (See Billing Instructions on Reverse)

7. TO: CONTRACTOR (Name, address, ZIP code)

8. DISCOUNT TERMS	10. TYPE OF ORDER SF 281 Code
	☐ A. PURCHASE–Reference your

9. DELIVER TO F.O.B. POINT ON OR BEFORE (Date)	Please furnish the following on the terms and conditions specified on both sides of this order and on the attached sheets, if any, including delivery as indicated.
	☐ B. DELIVERY–Except for billing instructions on the reverse, this delivery order is subject to instructions contained on this side only of this form and is issued subject to the terms and conditions of the above-numbered contract.

11. GOVERNMENT B/L NO.	12. F.O.B. POINT	13. PLACE OF INSPECTION AND ACCEPTANCE

14. SCHEDULE (See reverse for Rejections)

ITEM NO. (A)	SUPPLIES OR SERVICES (B)	QUANTITY ORDERED (C)	UNIT (D)	UNIT PRICE (E)	AMOUNT (F)	QUANTITY ACCEPTED (G)

15. BUSINESS CLASSIFICATION (Check appropriate boxes)

☐ SMALL ☐ OTHER THAN SMALL ☐ DISADVANTAGED 8(a) ☐ MINORITY ☐ WOMAN-OWNED ☐ LABOR SURPLUS ☐ INTER-AGENCY

14(H). TOTAL (Cont. pages)

16. ISSUING OFFICE (Address correspondence to) U.S. FISH AND WILDLIFE SERVICE

14(H) GRAND TOTAL

17. NAME AND WARRANT NUMBER OF CONTRACTING OFFICER (Typed)	18. UNITED STATES OF AMERICA BY (Signature)

FOR GOVERNMENT USE ONLY (See Note on Reverse)

ACCOUNTING LINE NO.	ORGN	FUND	BFY	SUB-ACTIVITY	PROJECT	OBJECT CLASS	DESCRIPTION ITEM NO. (Block 14A)	AMOUNT

FORM NO. 3-2103

Exhibit 4. Example of Completed Order for Supplies or Services

ORDER FOR SUPPLIES OR SERVICES

	Page	of	Pages

IMPORTANT: Mark all packages and papers with contract and/or order numbers.

1. DATE OF ORDER	2. REQUISITIONING OFFICE	3. CONTRACT NO. (if any)	4. ORDER NO.
3-18-91	National Elk Refuge		61550·91·00029

5. SHIP TO: (Consignee and address, ZIP code)

National Elk Refuge
Box C
Jackson, WY 83001

6. MAIL INVOICE IN TRIPLICATE TO: (Include ZIP code) (See Billing Instructions on Reverse)

National Elk Refuge
675 East Broadway
Jackson, WY 83001

7. TO: CONTRACTOR (Name, address, ZIP code)

UNICOR Sign Order Center
Data/Graphics Division
Room 126, 302 First St. N.W.
Washington, D.C. 20534

8. DISCOUNT TERMS	10. TYPE OF ORDER SF 281 Code
	☒ A. PURCHASE—Reference your

9. DELIVER TO F.O.B. POINT ON OR BEFORE (Date)

11-1-91

Please furnish the following on the terms and conditions specified on both sides of this order and on the attached sheets, if any, including delivery as indicated.

☐ B. DELIVERY—Except for billing instructions on the reverse, this delivery order is subject to instructions contained on this side only of this form and is issued subject to the terms and conditions of the above-numbered contract.

11. GOVERNMENT B/L NO.	12. F.O.B. POINT	13. PLACE OF INSPECTION AND ACCEPTANCE

14. SCHEDULE (See reverse for Rejections)

ITEM NO. (A)	SUPPLIES OR SERVICES (B)	QUANTITY ORDERED (C)	UNIT (D)	UNIT PRICE (E)	AMOUNT (F)	QUANTITY ACCEPTED (G)
	Standard Fish & Wildlife Service Area Management Signs (A-Series)					
1.	fws A·4 (Public Fishing Area)	6	ea.	7.25	43.50	
2.	fws A·5 (Public Hunting Area)	20	ea.	5.95	119.00	
3.	fws A·6 (Area Beyond This S:	200	ea.	5.25	1,050.00	
					1,212.50	

SAMPLE

15. BUSINESS CLASSIFICATION (Check appropriate box)						14(H). TOTAL (Cont. pages)
☐ SMALL	☐ OTHER THAN SMALL	☐ DISAD-VANTAGED 8(a)		...ABOR SURPLUS	☐ INTER-AGENCY	

16. ISSUING OFFICE (Address correspondence to) U.S. FISH A... ...RVICE National Elk Refuge Box C Jackson, WY 83001 $ 1,212.50

14(H) GRAND TOTAL

17. NAME AND WARRANT NUMBER OF CONTRACTING OFFICER (Typed)	18. UNITED STATES OF AMERICA BY (Signature)
JOHN SMITH # # #	

FOR GOVERNMENT USE ONLY (See Note on Reverse)

ACCOUNTING LINE NO.	ORGN	FUND	BFY	SUB-ACTIVITY	PROJECT	OBJECT CLASS	DESCRIPTION ITEM NO. (Block 14A)	AMOUNT

FORM NO. 3-2103

Exhibit 5. Post Detail

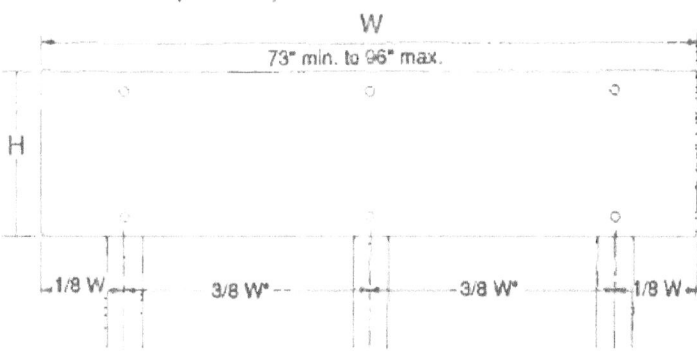

SINGLE-, TWO-, AND THREE-POST DETAIL

W
73" min. to 96" max.

H

1/8 W — 3/8 W" — 3/8 W" — 1/8 W

TYPICAL THREE-POST DETAIL

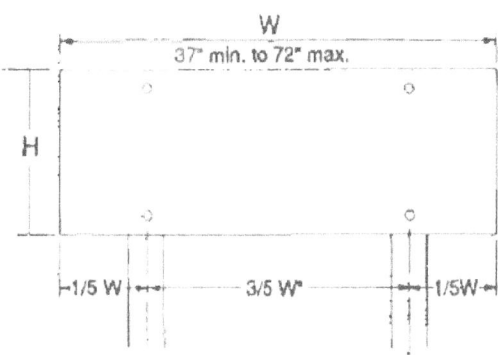

W
37" min. to 72" max.

H

1/5 W — 3/5 W" — 1/5 W

TYPICAL TWO-POST DETAIL

*This spacing applicable only for signs that are not predrilled.

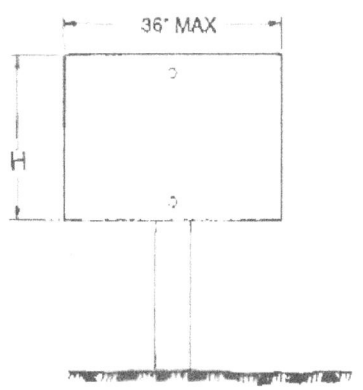

36" MAX

H

TYPICAL SINGLE-POST DETAIL

Legend
W = Width of Sign
H = Height of Sign

Typical Post Spacing and Maximum
Board Size Relationships for
Destination Guide Sign Installations

Exhibit 6. Wooden Breakaway Support Guidelines

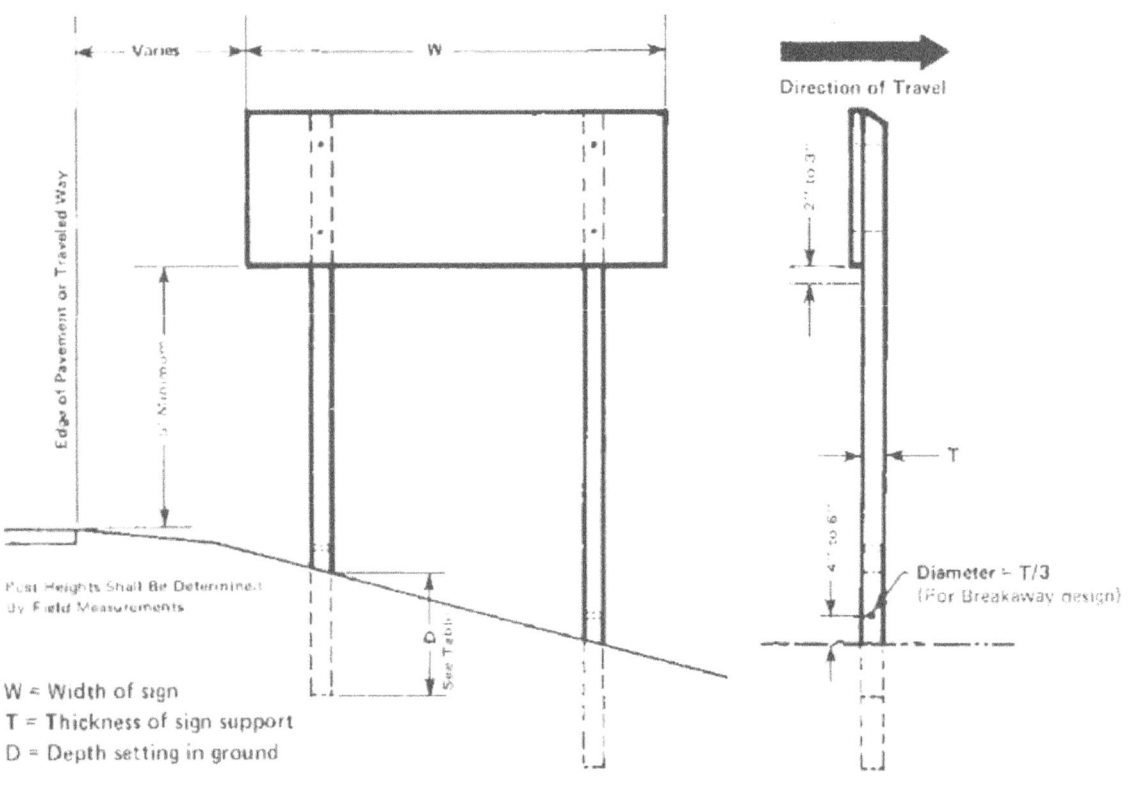

W = Width of sign
T = Thickness of sign support
D = Depth setting in ground

Post Heights Shall Be Determined By Field Measurements

Diameter = T/3 (For Breakaway design)

DOUBLE SUPPORT

Breakaway Design Post Sizes ...

Post size	"D" min.	Single post	Maximum sign area (sq ft)		
			Double post	Triple post	Quadruple post
4"x4"	3'	10*	20		
4"x6"	4'	15*	35	45	
6"x6"	4'	20**	50	75	100

* Use two 4"x4" posts if W is over 3'.
**Use two 4"x4" posts if W is over 4'.

Breakaway design is required for all posts (new and existing) with cross sectional area greater than 24 square inches. Use drilled hole at bottom of support only. Field drill posts and treat hole with preservative.

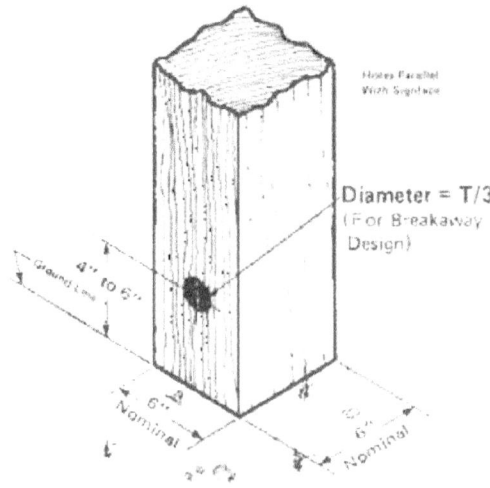

Diameter = T/3 (For Breakaway Design)

TYPICAL BREAKAWAY SUPPORT

Reducing Shear Resistance Without Substantial Loss Of Capacity To Withstand Wind Loading

Exhibit 7. Vandlgard Nut Assembly

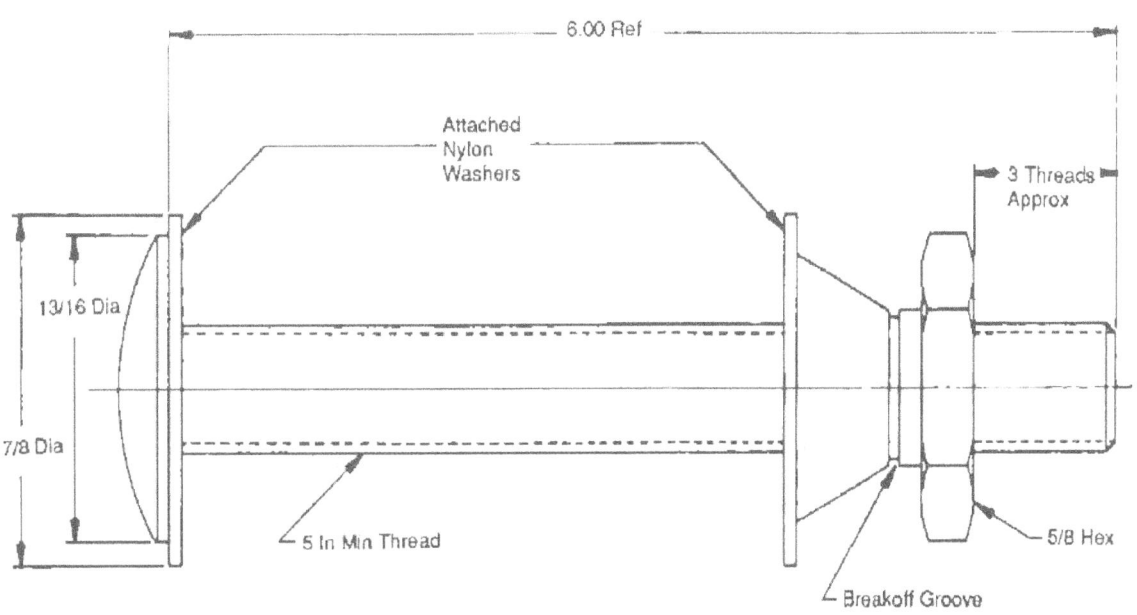

6.00 Ref

Attached Nylon Washers

3 Threads Approx

13/16 Dia

7/8 Dia

5 In Min Thread

5/8 Hex

Breakoff Groove

VANDLGARD-NUT—INSTALLATION AND REMOVAL

INSTALLATION

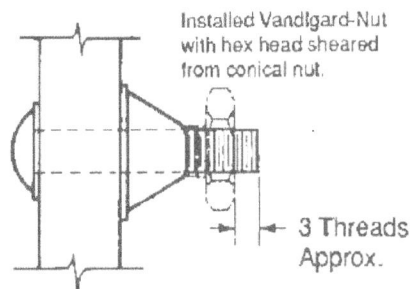

Installed Vandlgard-Nut with hex head sheared from conical nut.

3 Threads Approx.

1. Install Vandlgard nut by tightening hex until it shears.

REMOVAL

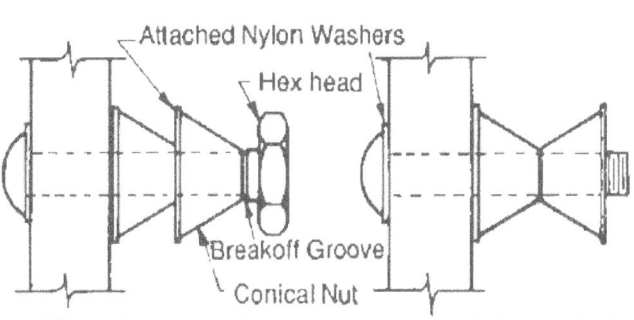

Attached Nylon Washers

Hex head

Breakoff Groove

Conical Nut

1. Thread on second Vandlgard and twist off hex. Remove the remaining conical nut.

2. Install this conical nut in the inverted position.

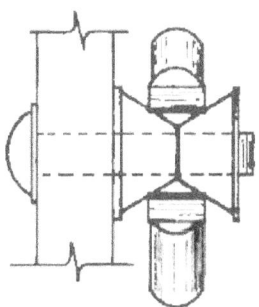

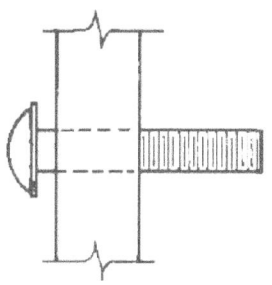

3. Squeeze both nuts firmly with vise-grips and remove both nuts together.

4. Original bolt is undamaged and ready for reuse.

Exhibit 7. Vandlgard Nut Assembly

VCN 138 COLOR CODE: GOLD

This standard series is designed for clamping metal to metal joints such as metal signs and posts. The high clamp-up (preload) assures a secure tamper resistant joint. Should be used with electroplated bolts. Because of the close thread tolerance, it cannot be used with hot dipped galvanized bolts. Available in UNC, UNF and metric thread sizes.

VCN 141 COLOR CODE: GREY

This nut is also designed for clamping metal to metal joints. It has the same high clamp-up as VCN 138. However, the nut is tapped with an oversize thread so that it may be used with hot dipped galvanized bolts. Available in 5/16-18, only.

VCN 145 COLOR CODE: GREEN

This nut is designed for clamping soft joints such as wood signs and posts. The low clamp-up is adequate for a secure joint yet in the case of traffic signs it will not compress the substrate or damage the reflective sheeting. Should be used with electroplated bolts. Because of the close thread tolerance, it cannot be used with hot dipped galvanized bolts.

VCN 150 COLOR CODE: NATURAL

This nut is functionally the same as the VCN 145 series but material is zinc rather than aluminum.

February 19, 1981

INSPECTION CHECKLIST

Name of Inspector

Field Station

Area

Sign No.   Description:

Date   Time:

	Substrate	Face (Overlay and Message)	Finish (Paint)	Sign Support	Braces	Hardware
Problem						
Cracking						
Ply Separation						
Scratching & Tears						
Blistering						
Missing						
Rotting						
Corrosion						
Unstable						
Dirty						
Poor Reflectivity						
Poor Visibility						
Recommendation						
Remove, Replace						
On-site Repair						
Shop Repair						
Apply Paint/Stain						
Stabilize						
Secure						
Clean						
Replace/Repaint Lettering						
Cut Brush or Grass						

REMARKS:

Exhibit 8. Example of Completed Inspection Checklist

INSPECTION CHECKLIST

Name of Inspector   JANE SMITH

Field Station   XY2 Refuge

Area   Fishing Pier

Sign No.   28   Description: Fishing Sign

Date   3·14·91   Time: 8:15 AM

	Substrate	Face (Overlay and Message)	Finish (Paint)	Sign Support	Braces	Hardware
Problem						
Cracking						
Ply Separation						
Scratching & Tears						
Blistering						
Missing						
Rotting				✓		
Corrosion						
Unstable						
Dirty		✓				
Poor Reflectivity						
Poor Visibility						
Recommendation						
Remove, Replace				✓ ①		
On-site Repair						
Shop Repair						
Apply Paint/Stain						
Stabilize						
Secure						
Clean		✓ ②				
Replace/Repaint Lettering						
Cut Brush or Grass	✓ ③					

REMARKS:

① Replace right support post

② Clean sign face

③ Trim brush along roadway in front of

SAMPLE

Chapter 4
Sign Maintenance

Chapter 4
Sign Maintenance

General

Proper sign maintenance is an important part of an effective sign program. Signs must be inspected and cleaned regularly and repaired, replaced, or removed when necessary, for the safety of visitors and employees and for cost-effective management. Missing, broken, or illegible signs can cause confusion and accidents. In addition, poor maintenance creates an appearance of neglect, which can lead to abuse and vandalism.

This section offers guidelines for maintaining sign panels, mountings, supports, and associated landscaping. Some specific procedures are outlined; however, field stations may use any safe procedures that accomplish the job and meet sign program objectives.

General Maintenance Tips

- Do not waste time and money repairing signs that do not comply with federal or Service standards. Instead replace them with appropriate signs or devices that do meet the standards.

- When maintaining roadside signs, be sure to use appropriate advance warning signs and devices to protect the safety of motorists and workers at each site. See Section VI of the MUTCD for more information on the kinds of signs and devices that may be used.

- Remember that careless maintenance can do more harm than good. The same high standards of workmanship should be applied to this task as to any other.

- When installing repaired or replacement signs, tighten bolts firmly but not too tight. Tightening bolts too tightly can rupture the reflective sheeting and the plywood. Place a nylon washer between the bolt head and the sign face to reduce the chance of rupturing the sign face.

- Use theft-resistant nuts (such as Vandlgard, as shown in Exhibit 7 on Page 3-23, or other similar nuts) when reinstalling signs.

- Remember that the maintenance of sign backs is also important and should be included as an element of total sign maintenance.

Sign Panel Maintenance

Storing Sign Panels

- Remove all packing material and slip sheeting so that nothing is against the sign face.

- Store signs upright, not lying down.

- Keep signs away from areas where they may get dirty or wet.

- Keep treated wood posts and other materials away from sign faces.

- Store signs inside. Adjustable square tubing or angle material makes a good storage rack for signs.

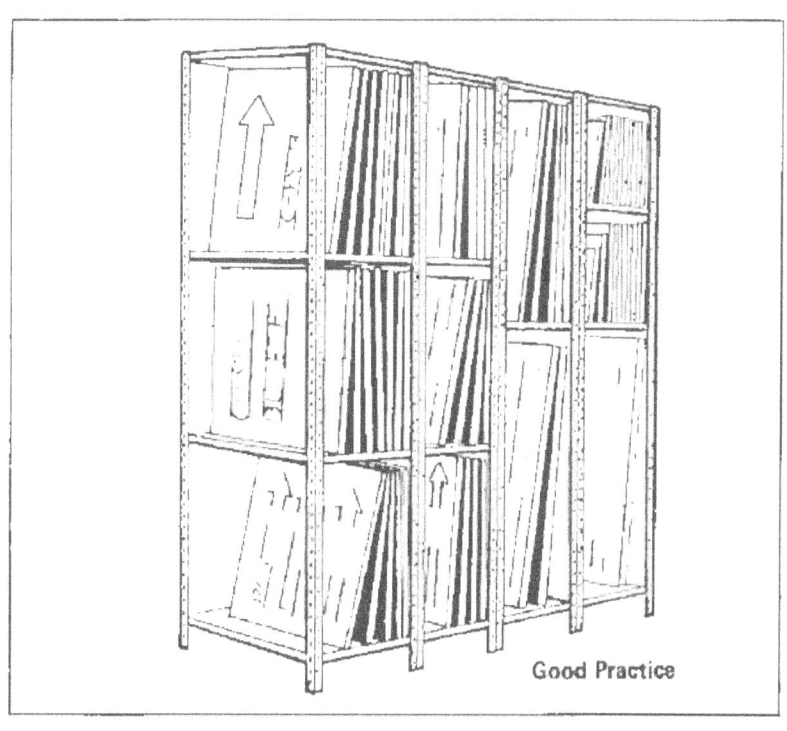

Good Practice

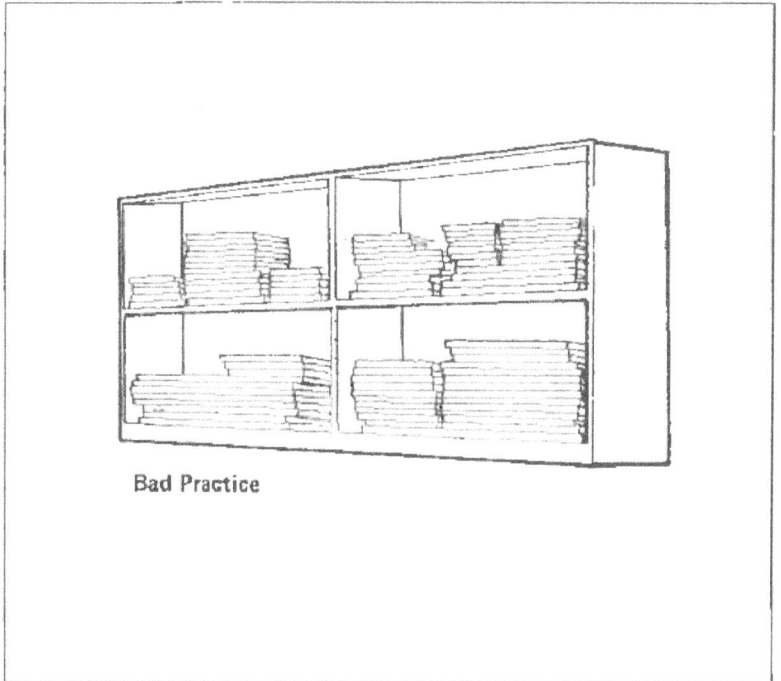

Bad Practice

Sign cleaning

Signs must be kept clean to ensure legibility. This is particularly true of reflective signs, which must be dirt-free for maximum readability. Signs should be cleaned with a non-abrasive detergent that is chemically neutral and does not contain strong aromatic solvents or alcohols. The steps to follow in cleaning sign faces are outlined below.

Cleaning Aluminum Signs and Plywood Signs

- Flush the sign surface with clean water to remove loose dirt.

- Wash the sign face with a soft brush, rag, or sponge using a mild, biodegradable detergent solution or other suitable cleaner.

- Wash sign panels from the top down; avoid scratching the panel surface with unnecessary scrubbing. If sign letters are applied (die cut and affixed) rather than silk-screened, wash them carefully to avoid loosening their edges.

- Rinse the entire sign face with clean water and allow it to dry thoroughly.

Cleaning Wood-routed Signs

Clean redwood and red cedar signs twice a year, or as needed with a mild biodegradable soap.

Removing Stains

Remove tar, oil, diesel smut, and bituminous material with a mild solvent, such as mineral spirits; follow with a mild, biodegradable detergent solution and clear water rinse. Lipstick and crayon can also be removed in this way.

A commercial aerosol carburetor/choke cleaner, available at most hardware and auto supply stores, can be used to remove paint from vandalized signs that are made with vinyl or reflective sheeting.

DO NOT use carburetor/choke cleaner on signs with painted backgrounds, such as Area Management signs, or signs with silk-screened copy. The carburetor choke/cleaner will dissolve most paints and silk-screen inks. **These products are flammable, so be sure to follow the safety precautions on the label. Material safety data sheets are available from product suppliers.**

Cleaning steps are outlined below:

1. Spray the painted (vandalized) area lightly with the carburetor/choke cleaner.

2. Wipe the dissolving paint with a cloth rag. The cleaner works very quickly.

3. Repeat steps 1 and 2 if needed. Several light applications are better than one heavy spraying.

4. Wash the sign with a mild, biodegradable detergent and rinse thoroughly with clean water to remove any remaining spray residue.

This procedure can be used on any sign with vinyl or reflective sheeting, regardless of substrate, since the cleaning substance is not likely to come into contact with the substrate. It can also be used to remove paint graffiti from concrete, rock, metal and other non-painted surfaces.

General

Determining whether a sign should be left as is, repaired, or replaced is a judgment usually made on-site at the sign location. Often it is cheaper to replace a badly damaged sign than to attempt extensive repairs. Compare the repair cost and the likely extended life of the sign with the new sign cost and expected life when deciding whether to repair or replace a sign.

In high-vandalism areas it may be wise to order several signs of the same kind at a time. The unit cost often goes down as the quantity goes up, and it may be cheaper in the long run to have replacement signs on hand than to spend a lot of time repairing signs.

Sign Repair Components

Field stations can order sign repair components (squeegee, reflective sheeting, aluminum foil tape, and die cut, pressure sensitive letters, numbers, and arrows) from the Winona Sign Shop and UNICOR. Regional sign coordinators can provide current prices for these items.

Bent Signs

Bent aluminum signs can often be repaired simply by straightening, provided the legend and background have not been scraped or severely damaged. If the legend or background is badly damaged, the sign should be replaced.

Bullet Holes and Punctures

It is not always necessary to repair every hole in a sign. When a hole is small, does not damage the message or symbol, and does not by itself create a poor image for the Service, consider the cost/benefit when deciding whether repair is necessary. When repairs are necessary, follow the guidelines below for the kind of sign being repaired.

1. Remove all damaged background sheeting and legend.

2. Straighten the sign using a hammer and flat dolly.

3. Remove any additional sheeting damaged during straightening.

4. Clean the entire area with mineral spirits, then with isopropyl alcohol.

5. Patch the bullet hole or puncture on both sides using aluminum foil tape. Apply firm pressure with a squeegee on both sides of the sign. On large holes start the foil strips at the bottom of the hole and work up, overlapping the strips shingle-fashion.

6. Apply pressure sensitive reflective background sheeting, extending it at least 1/2 inch beyond the foil tape strips.

7. Replace damaged legend, borders, and symbols.

8. If the sign is subject to snow burial and replacement sheeting extends to the top edge of the sign, place transparent film along the top edge.

9. It is usually not cost effective to repair small aluminum signs.

Reflectorized Plywood Signs

1. Remove loose wood on both sides of the sign and all damaged sheeting.

2. Use an exterior wood filler. The new latex compounds will also work. Always read manufacturer's instructions before using cleaning products on vinyl type signs.

3. Place a piece of ordinary household waxed paper over the putty.

4. Using a straight edge or a putty knife, press down and smooth the putty.

5. After the putty has dried (usually about 15 minutes), sand the patch smooth with a belt sander.

6. Patch the bullet hole or puncture on both sides using aluminum foil tape. Apply firm pressure with a squeegee on both sides of the sign. On large holes start the foil strips at the bottom of the hole and work up, overlapping the strips shingle-fashion.

7. Wipe the area with a clean cloth.

8. Apply pressure-sensitive reflective background sheeting, extending it at least 1/2 inch beyond the patch.

9. Replace damaged legends, borders, and symbols.

10. If the sign is subject to snow burial, and replacement sheeting extends to the top edge of the sign, place transparent film along the top edge.

11. Use an aerosol can of flat black enamel, lightly spray the aluminum foil tape covering the holes on the sign back. Keep the paint off the sign face because it destroys reflectivity.

Replacing Vinyl Sheeting and Legends

Minor scratches or small holes in signs with vinyl faces, either aluminum-backed or plywood-backed, can be repaired with pressure-sensitive sheeting, which comes in pieces or rolls and is available through the authorized sign procurement sources (currently Winona Sign Shop and UNICOR). If there is extensive damage to a sign's vinyl sheeting, the sign should be replaced rather than repaired.

Reflective sheeting loses its reflectivity over time and has a shelf life of approximately 1-2 years when stored away from light and heat. Therefore, it is not practical or cost effective to order it in quantities and store it for long periods.

Follow these steps to replace sections of vinyl sheeting:

1. Remove the background sheeting from an area slightly larger than that damaged.

   -- Clean the area around the damaged portion of the sign.

   - **Very carefully** heat the section to be removed using a heat gun or heat lamp.

   - work a sharp, beveled putty knife under the edge of the sheeting and strip it from the adhesive. Remove all sheeting loosened by heat.

2. Clean the surface again with mineral spirits, then with isopropyl alcohol. Apply new reflective sheeting as follows:

   - Separate the sheeting from the liner slightly at one corner or edge.

   - Place sheeting face down on a clean, dust-free surface and remove the liner. If the temperature is below 50 degrees

Fahrenheit, activate the adhesive with a heat activator. If possible, do this work in a heated shop when outside temperatures are less than 50 degrees F.

— Gently position the sheeting correctly on the surface being repaired, overlapping the surrounding sheeting to prevent premature sticking. Tack the sheet in place by finger pressure at two points on the upper edge, then press it firmly to the surface with a squeegee. Use overlapping strokes, starting at the center and working out to the edges. Initial squeegee pressure must be very firm to avoid forming air pockets near the upper corner. Lift the upper corners back beyond the points at which the sheet was tacked to the surface to prevent wrinkles at the tack points as the application proceeds to the edges.

— Squeegee the edges again using very firm pressure, and then wipe the face of the patch sheeting with a soft cloth to remove any surface dust.

— If the sign is subject to snow burial, and replacement sheeting extends to the top edge of the sign, place transparent film along the top edge.

3. Once the reflective sheeting has been applied, replace the damaged legend using the following steps:

— Mark a light, straight, horizontal line on the sign to guide the top alignment of the legend, border, or symbol.

— Lay the first character on a flat surface and carefully remove the protective liner.

- Align the top edge of the first character with the guide line, press the edge down, then press the rest of the character carefully and firmly in place.
- Squeegee the character down firmly.
- Align each additional character with the horizontal guide line and the right edge of the last character, and then press the new character onto the surface.

Repairing Wood-Routed Signs

1. Clean the damaged area.

2. Use an exterior wood filler or one of the new latex compounds.

3. Place a piece of ordinary household waxed paper over the putty.

4. Using a straight edge or a putty knife, press down and smooth the putty.

5. After the putty has dried (usually about 15 minutes), sand the patch smooth.

6. Pencil in the outline of any damaged text.

7. Reroute the message, using a router bit of the same width and depth as the original routing.

8. Repaint the message, first with a primer/sealer. Let dry, then apply enamel paint, using an artist's brush.

9. After the message enamel has dried, the sign face and back can be repainted or refinished.

Wood Signs

When repainting signs, use ready-mixed, exterior type polysilicone alkyd resin-base enamel, conforming to Federal Specification TT-E-I 593B. Colors must conform to Federal Specification 595a as follows:

Color	Federal Specification 595a No.
Brown	20059
Yellow-Cream	23695
Yellow	13767
Orange	12473
White	27875
Light Blue	15193
Black	17038
Green	14260
Tan	20260
Salmon Pink	22356
Seminole Brown (standard redwood color)	20109

Before repainting or refinishing the background of wood routed signs, repair any holes in the message portion of the sign as outlined above.

The following tips may be helpful in applying the paint or stain:

- Use a 1/8-inch-thick polysponge roller (standard fabric rollers may spread the paint or stain into the routed area).

- Avoid getting too much paint or stain on the roller.

- Use light pressure on the sign surface.

- Move the roller in a crisscross pattern to speed coverage.

- Eliminate any bubbles by rolling the surface with a dry polysponge roller.

Reflectorized Plywood Signs

When repainting the back of a reflectorized plywood sign, take care not to get paint or finishing agents on the front of the sign panel because they damage the reflective surface.

- Inspect all hardware, including bolts, nuts, washers, and other fasteners, to ensure that they are tight and free from corrosion and damage.

- Replace missing, damaged, and corroded hardware and tighten loose bolts and fasteners.

- Use theft-resistant nuts (such as Vandlgard) when installing signs.

- Where hardware is visible, you may wish to paint the head of the bolt to match the sign face and the nut to match the supports. The Vandlgard nut assembly is available in green, grey, gold, and natural zinc colors. The colors represent specific applications for the hardware; (e.g. green = wood to wood and will shear when enough torque is applied, gold = metal to metal, etc.).

- Tighten bolts firmly, but not too tight when securing soft materials such as plywood. Tightening bolts too tight can rupture the reflective sheeting and the plywood overlay. The Vandlgard nut (shown in Exhibit 1) is designed for clamping soft joints such as wood signs and posts. When proper torque is reached while tightening the nut, the bolt will shear off before the washer or bolt head is pulled into the sign face.

- Place a nylon washer (supplied in Vandlgard nut assemblies) between the bolt head and the sign face to reduce the chances of rupturing the sign face.

- Sign supports that are not plumb should be straightened. Cracked or damaged supports should be replaced as soon as possible.

Ground Maintenance

Sign faces must be kept clear of obstructing weeds, trees, shrubbery, and construction materials. Landscaping around signs should not detract from the signs and should be in harmony with the surrounding environment, be it natural or man-made.

Vandalism

The problem of vandalism cannot be overlooked in a sign maintenance program. Defacement and destruction of signs occur on all Service lands. Vandalism ranges from scribblings, gunshots, and painting to outright theft. The following steps are recommended to help reduce vandalism:

- Use materials that continue to perform the sign function even when marred. For example, a plywood or routed wood substrate reduces the effect of bullet damage (when bullets enter the face of the sign).

- Use vandal-resistant hardware to prevent signs from being easily loosened and carried away.

- Use anchor rods or cleats at the bottom of the signpost to prevent its rotation or removal.

- Place signs that must be close to the roadway at the maximum practical mounting height. Do not locate signs near pullouts if it can be legally avoided. Careful site consideration will accomplish the signing need while minimizing vandalism.

- Place signs as far from the edge of the pavement as practical/possible.

- Make repairs or replacements promptly. A demonstration of resolve on the part of the Service may eventually wear down persistent vandals.

- Negatively worded signs are more frequently targeted for vandalism than positive signs.

- The authorized sign manufacturer will affix the maker's mark on the back of the sign at the time of manufacture to identify it as an official device. This aids in prosecuting vandals.

Chapter 5
Catalog

Chapter 5
Catalog

ENTRANCE SIGNS

Entrance signs are used to identify Service lands. They will be placed at major public entrance roads on all refuges, fish hatcheries, and research facilities.

Description

The standard Service entrance sign will be manufactured in 1 1/2" cedar, redwood, high density overlay (HDO) 3/4" plywood, or other suitable substrate. Considerations in selecting the substrate will be purchase and maintenance costs, suitability to a given climate, appearance, and appropriateness of the medium for the political climate of the area (e.g. using redwood when spotted owl populations are declining). If dimensional lumber is used, the sign may be either routed or sandblasted. If HDO plywood is used, the face of the sign will be covered with vinyl sheeting and die cut letters will be used.

Standard entrance signs will be either 4' X 8' or 5' X 10'. Corners will be rounded on a 3" radius.

The signs will have redwood colored background with buff colored letters. Letters will be in either the Oracle Medium or Optima Medium type styles. Type will be in upper and lower case letters, with upper case used for initial capital letters of the facility name and Service branch. Size of the letters will be dictated by vehicle speed standards, and by the size of the sign.

The Service emblem will be the sole graphic element on all standard entrance signs. The emblem will be in full color porcelain on enameled steel for the routed and sandblasted signs, and on full color vinyl for the vinyl-faced signs.

Complete specifications for Service entrance signs are available through Regional Sign Coordinators.

Installation And Mounting

Clearance
For the safety of motorists, entrance signs should be placed as far from the road as practical. Twelve feet from the edge of the traveled way is the minimum distance allowable in most instances.

Normally, signs should be posted so the lower edge is 5 feet above ground level. Where the sign might be blocked from view, it may be posted up to 7 feet above the level of the ground.

Posts
The standard base for Entrance Signs will consist of treated wood posts, but bases and skirts may be constructed of other materials such as brick, fieldstone, masonry, or wood. Signs placed within 30 feet of a public roadway should conform to the breakaway specifications described on page 3-22.

Entrance signs should be mounted using 1/4" aluminum angle, attached to the sign back with #10 X 7/8" maximum stainless steel sheet metal screws spaced 6" on center. Vandal-resistant hardware will be used to attach the Service emblems. A 6" x 6" CCA-treated wood post, number 2 or better, well-seasoned and free of defects, is considered standard.

Ordering
Orders for the Service entrance sign will be made through the Regional Sign Coordinator, using the Custom Sign Order Form, found on page 3-14.

This sign will be suitable for most Service facilities. However, for those cases in which the standard sign may be inappropriate, a project leader may order custom entrance signs by obtaining, in writing, concurrence from his/her supervisor, the Regional Sign Coordinator, and the Regional Director.

VERTICAL SIGNS

5 × 10 FORMAT

5 × 10 FORMAT WITH SKIRTING

4 × 8 FORMAT

4 × 8 FORMAT WITH SKIRTING

HORIZONTAL SIGNS

5 × 10 FORMAT

4 × 8 FORMAT

5 × 10 FORMAT
WITH SKIRTING

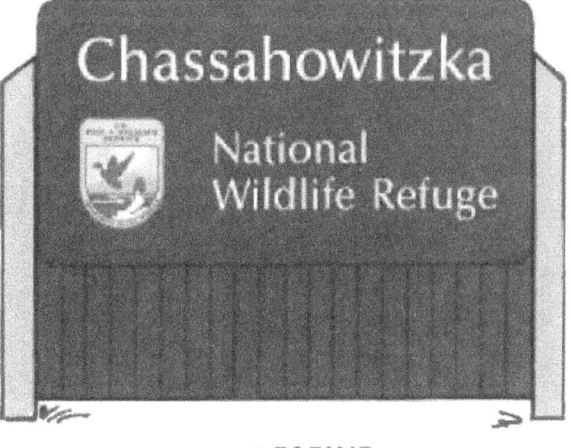

4 × 8 FORMAT
WITH SKIRTING

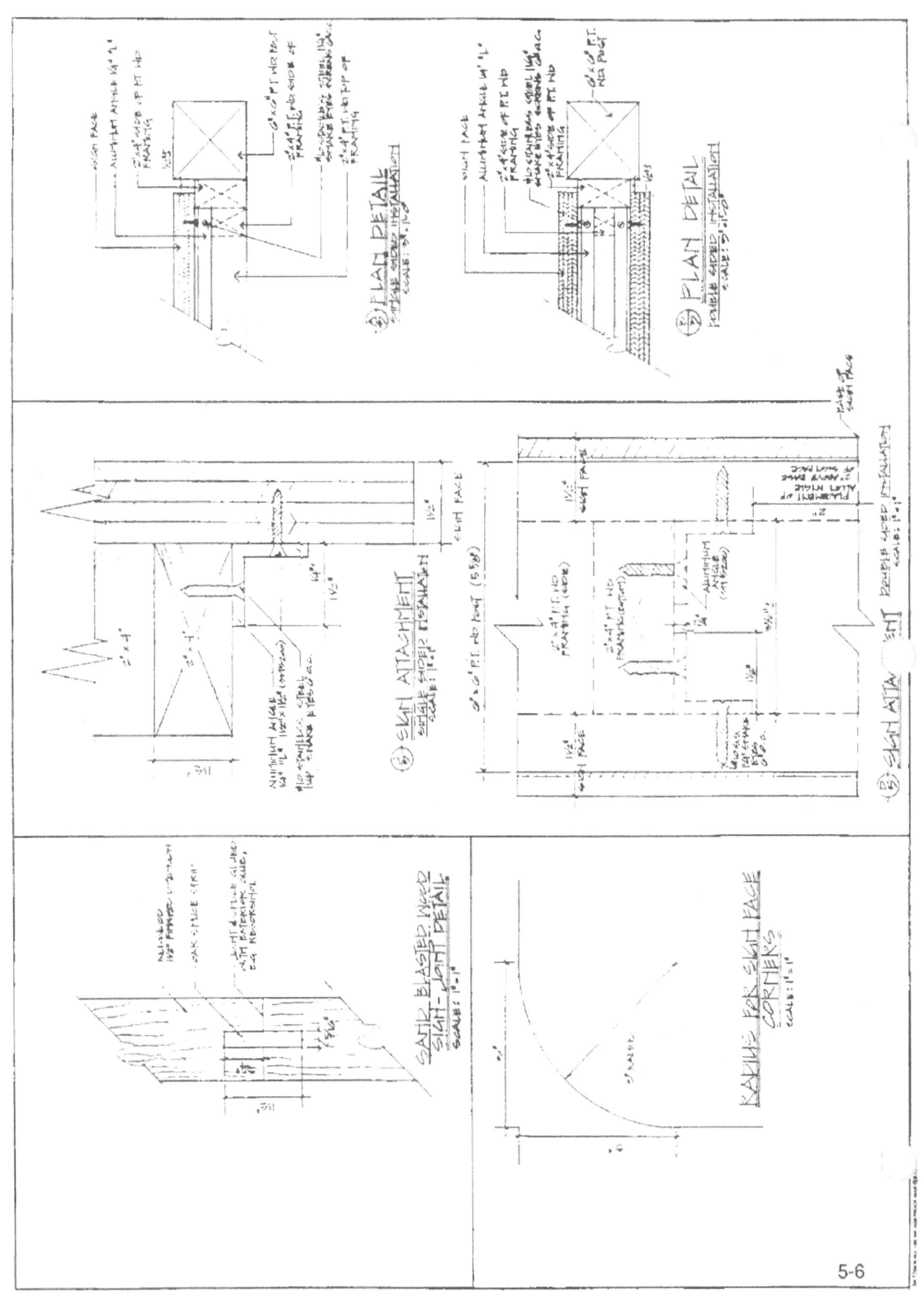

5-6

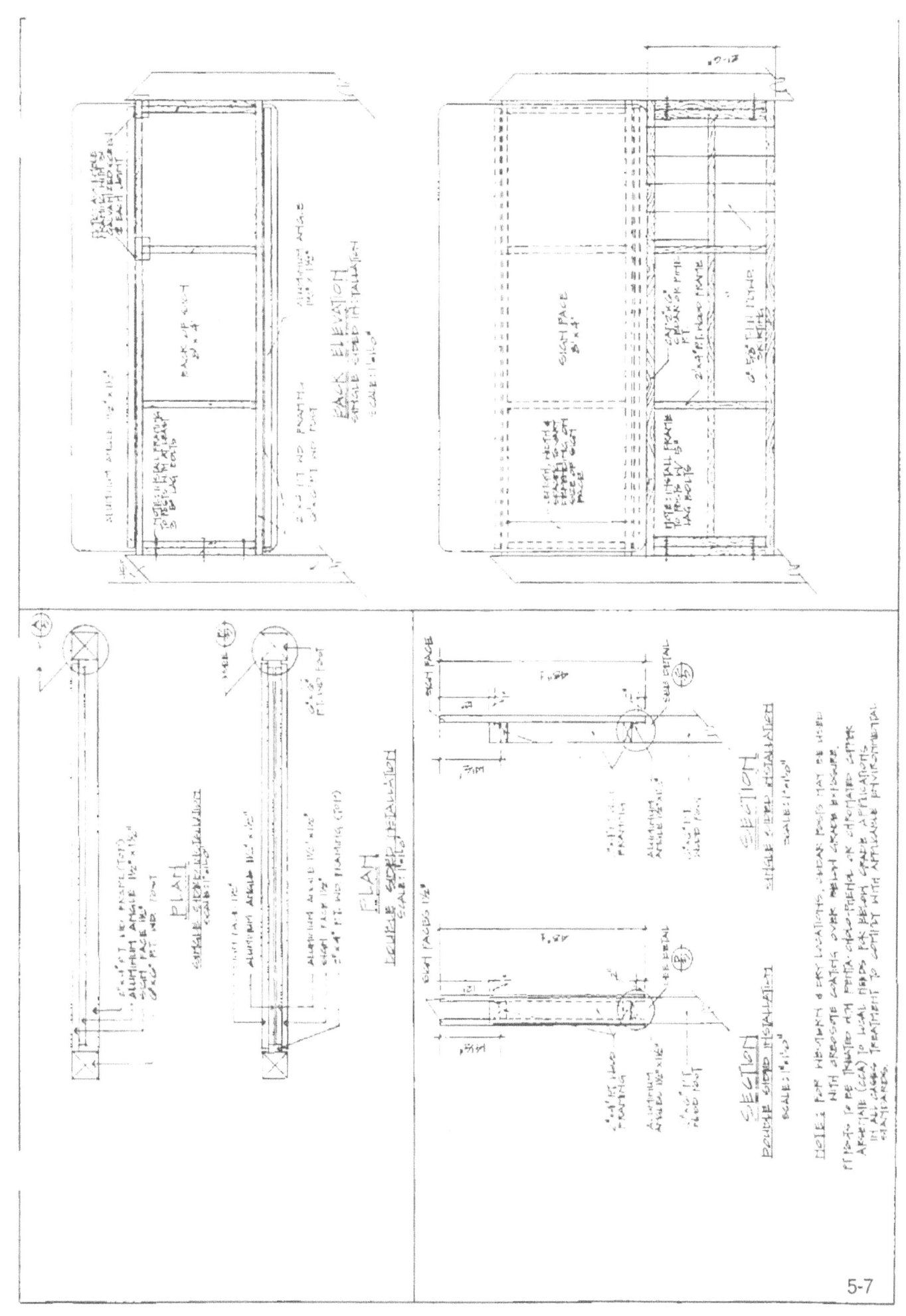

5-7

Ready Reference Guide To Area Management Signs

	Boundary Signs	Designated Area Signs
Use	Mark boundaries at: • Research Areas • National Fish Hatcheries • National Wildlife Refuges • Waterfowl Production Areas • Conservation Easements • Other Service Lands	Mark: • Areas designated for special use • Areas where specific activities are permitted/prohibited • Significant projects of the Youth Conservation Corps
Description	Aluminum, non-reflective Baked enamel paint background with silk screened legend 11" x 14" signs have mounting holes predrilled, 3/8" diameter, 12" apart.	
Placement	Place on boundary lines so they are visible from one to another, no more than 1/4 mile apart. Corners and entry points should be clearly marked with two signs. When used with another sign, place boundary marker above other sign. When placed along public access roads, place as far from the road as practical ! usually 12 feet.	Place so they are visible from one to another, no more than 1/4 mile apart where necessary to: • Identify areas designated for special uses. • Inform visitors of permitted and prohibited activities or special regulations in effect When placed at a boundary, post the Designated Area sign below the Boundary sign.
Mounting and Installation	Generally, mount on 4" x 4" CCA-treated wood Mounting posts; metal (or in some situations, other approved materials) may be used in remote areas with little public use or when replacing a sign that was on a metal post that was in good condition. Mount so lower edge is 5 feet above ground level. Mount using vandal-resistant hardware. When installing within 30 feet of public access roads, mount on breakaway posts unless the sign is protected by a guardrail or topographic change. (Wood 4" x 4" posts and standard U-channel steel posts do not require breakaway treatment.	
Ordering	Order from UNICOR by code number on Purchase Order (3-2103) Submit to Regional Sign Coordinator for approval unless direct ordering is authorized.	
Maintenance	Clean and inspect regularly. Wash with a mild, biodegradable detergent and water solution. Replace damaged signs.	

AREA MANAGEMENT SIGNS

General

Area management signs are designed to facilitate managing Service lands. They mark boundaries, identify special areas or functions of specific areas, and describe permitted and prohibited activities.

Description

Area Management signs are aluminum, non-reflective signs. They have a baked enamel paint background and a silk-screened legend. Most area management signs measure 11" x 14". The 11' x 14" signs have mounting holes predrilled 3/8 inch in diameter, 12 inches apart. All Area Management signs are standard signs and cannot be altered. They are ordered by their Service code number.

Installation and Mounting

Clearance

For the safety of motorists, Area Management signs posted along public-access roads should be placed as far from the road as practical. Twelve feet from the edge of the traveled way is the minimum distance allowable in most instances.

Normally, signs should be posted so the lower edge is 5 feet above ground level. Where the sign might be blocked from view (by pedestrians, for instance), it should be 7 feet above the level of the ground. Where two signs are mounted on one post, the bottom of the lower sign may be lower than specified above. (See pages 3-8 through 3-9).

Posts

Generally, Area Management signs should be mounted using vandal-resistant hardware on wood posts. A 4" x 4" CCA-treated wood post, number 2 or better, well-seasoned and free of defects, is considered standard. However, metal posts are acceptable in these instances:

- Use in remote areas not generally visited by the public, such as Boundary signs in remote areas.

- Replacement of a sign previously mounted on a metal post that is still in good condition.

If metal posts are used within 30 feet of a public-access road, they should be of breakaway design. The standard wood 4"x4" post, standard U-channel, and 2" tubular metal posts are small enough not to require breakaway design.

Ordering

See Appendix 3 for ordering information on Service Area Management Signs.

In accordance with 18 USC 4124, Area Management signs must be purchased from UNICOR. They can be ordered by code number on standard Purchase Order forms (3-2103). Orders should be submitted to the Regional sign coordinator for processing. Generally, larger orders allow for price reductions per unit. Regional sign coordinators may, at their discretion, waive the requirement for Regional approval and authorize field station managers to submit their purchase orders for Area Management signs directly to UNICOR.

Maintenance

Cleaning and Repair

Area Management signs should be cleaned and inspected regularly. They can be washed with a mild, biodegradable detergent and water solution. Cleaners with solvents or abrasives would damage the baked enamel background and should not be used. When Area Management signs are damaged, it is usually more cost effective to replace them than to repair them.

Replacement

Visibility is a consideration in deciding whether to replace a sign. In remote areas, away from general public view, signs can be left in place as long as they are fulfilling their purpose. Minor damage or rust can be overlooked as long as the sign is fully legible and intact. In areas having more public use, signs should be replaced if their overall appearance does not convey a positive image of the Service. More information on sign maintenance can be found on pages 4-1 through 4-5 of this manual.

Information on the uses, colors, and special considerations relating to the different Area Management signs is found on the pages that follow.

Boundary Signs

Placement

All Boundary signs should be installed on boundary lines so they are visible from one to another or at intervals no greater than 1/4 mile.

Corners and entry points should be clearly marked with two signs, one facing each direction.

Boundary signs should never be placed under other signs. If another sign is needed at a boundary (Area Closed, Public Hunting Area, etc.), the supplementary sign should be placed below the Boundary sign with a 1-inch space between the signs. No more than two signs should be placed on a post.

Additional information applying to Boundary signs can be found on the following pages of this manual:

- Mounting, page 3-6

- Ordering, page 3-1

- Maintenance, page 4-1

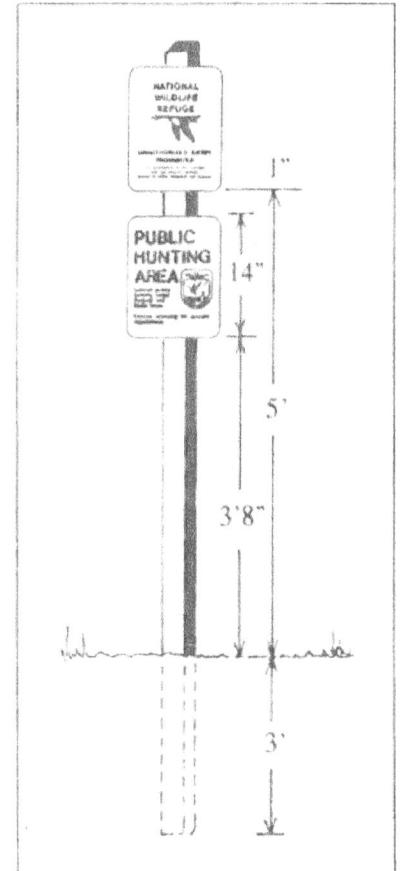

Information on each specific type of Boundary sign can be found on the following pages.

Types of Boundary Signs

U.S. Fish And Wildlife Service Boundary Sign (FWS-A-1)

U.S. Fish and Wildlife Service (Service) Boundary signs are used to mark the boundaries of research areas, fish hatcheries, and Alaska national wildlife refuges.

National Wildlife Refuge Boundary Sign (FWS-A-2)

National Wildlife Refuge Boundary Signs are used to mark the boundaries of all national wildlife refuges except those in Alaska. They carry the message that unauthorized entry is prohibited, which is not applicable for Alaskan refuges since their boundaries have been legally designated as open. The Service Boundary sign (FWS-A-l) is used to designate the boundaries on Alaskan Refuges.

Refuge managers should use good judgement when placing Boundary signs. For example, Boundary signs with Unauthorized Entry Prohibited should not be placed directly adjacent to trailheads or entrances to boardwalks.

WATERFOWL PRODUCTION AREA

OPEN
TO PUBLIC HUNTING

U. S. DEPARTMENT OF THE INTERIOR
FISH AND WILDLIFE SERVICE

CONSERVATION

EASEMENT

BOUNDARY

U.S. Fish and Wildlife Service

Sign is 3" x 4½"

Waterfowl Production Area Boundary Sign (FWS-A-3)

Waterfowl Production Area Boundary Signs mark the boundaries of areas that have been legally designated as Waterfowl Production Areas.

Conservation Easement Boundary Sign (FWS-A-18)

Conservation Easement Boundary Signs mark the boundaries of conservation easements acquired through the Farmers Home Administration. These signs are meant only to show the Service and the landowner/tenant where the boundary lines are, and should be used alone where easements without management interests are acquired. For those easements where there is a need to inform the public (e.g. the area is open/closed to hunting), additional existing standard signs and posts will be required.

Designated Area Signs

Placement

Designated Area Signs should be installed so they are visible from one to another, no more than 1/4 mile apart where appropriate to:

- Identify areas designated for special use.
- Inform visitors of permitted and prohibited activities or special regulations in effect.
- Advise of the necessity to consult the manager for further information.
- Mark significant projects of the Youth Conservation Corps.

Where a Designated Area Sign is used at a boundary, it is considered supplementary to the Boundary Sign and is posted 1 inch below it. No more than two signs should be placed on one post.

Additional information applying to Designated Area Signs can be found on the following pages of this manual:

- Mounting, page 3-6
- Ordering, page 3-1
- Maintenance, page 4-1

Types of Designated Area Signs

Public Fishing Area Sign (FWS-A-4)

Public Fishing Area signs are used to inform the public that limited sport fishing is permitted in the designated area.

Public Hunting Area Sign (FWS-A-5)

Public Hunting Area signs are used to inform the public that limited sport hunting is permitted in the designated area.

Area Beyond This Sign Closed Sign (FWS-A-6)

Area Closed Signs are used to inform the public that the designated area is closed to all entry.

Area Closed To Pursuing, Hunting Migratory Birds Sign (FWS-A-7)

Area Closed to Hunting Migratory Birds Signs are used in areas designated by Presidential Proclamation or Executive Order as being closed to migratory bird hunting, primarily when those areas fall within national wildlife refuge boundaries.

Areas so designated are listed in Title 50 of the Code of Federal Regulations, Subsection 32.4, as cited on the sign. These designated areas (lands and waters) may be located within, adjacent to, or in the vicinity of a national wildlife refuge. The signs should not be used in areas other than those listed in Subsection 32.4. In addition, these signs cannot be posted on non-Service lands without a formal agreement between the Service and the rightful property owner(s).

Notice–Government Property Sign (FWS-A-8)

Notice-Government Property Signs are used to identify select government property (outbuildings, maintenance sheds, etc.) and to inform the public that no trespassing is permitted in the designated area.

No Hunting Zone Sign (FWS-A-9)

No Hunting Zone Signs are used to inform the public that no hunting is permitted in the designated area. These signs are used for safety purposes and may be posted around hunter check stations, hunter parking areas, and other areas within a designated hunting area. They may also be posted along fish hatchery boundaries if hunting pressures are significant and hunter trespassing has been a problem.

Pheasant Hunting Only Sign (FWS-A-10)

Pheasant Hunting Only Signs are used to inform the public that only pheasant hunting is permitted in the designated area.

Waterfowl Hunting Only Sign (FWS-A-11)

Waterfowl Hunting Only Signs are used to inform the public that only waterfowl hunting is permitted in the designated area.

Spaced Blind Area Sign (FWS-A-12)

Spaced Blind Area Signs are used to inform the public that the hunting area is restricted and that hunters are assigned to sites.

Steel Shot Zone Sign (FWS-A-13)

This sign is used to inform the public that steel shot ammunition is required in the designated hunting area.

National Wilderness Area Sign (FWS-A-14)

National Wilderness Area Signs are used to inform the public that the area has been designated by Congress as a National Wilderness Area.

National Wild And Scenic River System Sign (FWS-A-15)

National Wild and Scenic River System Signs are used to inform the public that the area has been designated by Congress as part of the National Wild and Scenic River System.

Youth Conservation Corps (date) Sign (FWS-A-16)

Youth Conservation Corps Signs are used to identify significant Youth Conservation Corps projects and the year of their completion.

Archaeological Site Sign (FWS-A-17)

Archaeological Site Signs are used to mark archaeological sites, which are protected by regulations.

In making decisions concerning the placement of this sign, field station managers should consider such factors as the public visibility of the site and the sensitivity of its cultural values. Placing signs in areas containing some types of archaeological sites may result in unnecessary recognition, which could lead to vandalism or unauthorized removal of artifacts. In these instances, it may be better to post a Notice - Government Property Sign (FWS-A-8) at the site.

In addition, there may be cases involving the protection of historic structures of recent periods when use of the Notice–Government Property Sign is more appropriate. Field station managers are encouraged to discuss the use and placement of signs with the Regional historic preservation officer to ensure maximum site protection. Refer to the Cultural Resource Management chapter of the Service's Refuge Manual (SRM 16) for additional information on the use of signs as protective measures.

OTHER AREA MANAGEMENT SIGNS
(FWS-A-19 - FWS-A-22)

The following are classified as Other Area Management Signs:

- FWS-A-21 Duck Stamp Recognition Sign

- FWS-A-22 Buckle Up

- FWS-A-19 100 Year Flood Level

- FWS-A-20 Flood of Record

These signs can be ordered from UNICOR by code number.

Ready Reference Guide to Information Signs

	General Information	Concession Area	Building Designation
Use	Inform visitors of: • Opportunities • Services • Regulations	Identify concession operations and provide information on: • goods and services • rates or fees • hours of operation	Identify buildings and sometimes show their hours of operation
Description	¾" HDO-plywood substrate covered with reflectorized vinyl sheeting White reflective letters on brown reflective background		
Design Standards	Sign size and letter height are determined by whether the sign is for motorist or pedestrian viewing and viewing distance Letter size is Helvetica medium U.S. Fee Symbol is used when appropriate Messages generally have flush left margins but may be centered when appropriate No more than 4 messages per sign Signs should not be placed where they will create distractions, obstructions, or hazards Signs meant for pedestrian viewing should be placed at an appropriate height		Letter size is Helvetica medium
Placement	Signs posted along public access roads should generally be at least 12' from the edge of the travelled way MUTCD guidelines should be followed when posting these signs for motorist viewing		Place at eye level on front exterior wall or along building's approach walk
Mounting and Installation	Signs posted for motorist viewing should be mounted 5' above the level of the road Most information signs can be mounted on standard 4" x 4" or 4" x 6" posts Mount using vandal-resistant hardware. If larger-than-standards posts are used, they must be of breakaway design unless the sign is protected by a guardrail or topographic change		If wall mounted, use rust-proof hardware appropriate to building materials If post mounted, use vandal-resistant hardware
Ordering	Order from UNICOR using the Service Custom Sign Order Form (FWS-3-2040)		
Maintenance	Inspect and clean regularly Wash with a mild, biodegradable detergent and water solution If a sign is vandalized or otherwise damaged, weigh the cost of repair in time and materials against the cost of a replacement sign Replace badly damaged signs		

INFORMATION SIGNS

Functions and Types of Information Signs

Information Signs inform visitors of services, opportunities, and regulations at the station. This section is divided into three parts:

- General Information Signs
- Concession Area Signs
- Building Designation Signs

To a great extent, the same general guidelines for design, placement, mounting, ordering, and maintenance apply to General Information, Concession Area, and Building Designation Signs. To avoid unnecessary repetition, these guidelines have been consolidated. The information that follows applies to each of these sign categories except as noted.

Design Standards

These design standards apply to the size and layout of General Information and Concession Area Signs. Sign size varies according to the size of the letters and the amount of text. Signs intended for pedestrian viewing use smaller lettering and are generally smaller in overall size. If the sign is to be read from moving vehicles, letter size is determined by traffic speed on the road where the sign is posted and/or the distance from which it will be viewed. Helvetica medium is the letter style, and both upper and lower case letters are used.

Usually, the overall size of a sign is determined by the manufacturer unless there is a particular reason for the station to determine it. For instance, if there is minimum space for the sign or if the sign is to be subordinate to another sign, the station may request a certain size sign.

The text on Information and Concession Area Signs is called the message(s). Guidelines for developing sign messages include the following:

- A single message should convey a single thought.

- Messages should:

  - contain only essential information.
  - be brief and simple.
  - present the most important information first.
  - identify station areas, offices, buildings, and features consistently (by the same name or title) throughout a field station.

- Generally, there should be no more than four messages on a sign.

An area name or title may appear in reverse color (brown text on white background) at the top of the sign, in larger letters than the text in the lower portion. If this style of General Information or Concession Area Sign is chosen, it should be used on all such signs at a facility and should be consistent in style and format.

Other options available on Information Signs include:

- removable panels for use where hours, fees, or regulations are subject to regular seasonal or periodic change.

- distribution boxes for making brochures available. (Signs holding brochures should not be posted along road where people need to stop their cars in a roadway to get a brochure. They should be located on pull-outs, near parking lots, or in other areas for pedestrian access).

Placement

Information Signs should be placed where they are needed, and overuse should be avoided. Further guidelines include:

- Signs should not be placed where they might create distractions, obstructions, or hazards.

- Signs meant for pedestrian viewing should be placed at eye level (about 5' 5").

- Larger signs posted for viewing at greater distances can be placed proportionately higher.

- Signs posted along roads should generally be at least 12 feet from the edge of the traveled way.

- Signs listing permitted and prohibited activities should be placed at least 100 feet apart.

Most Information Signs can be mounted on standard 4"x 4" or 4" x 6" CCA-treated wood posts. Use of standard posts eliminates the need for breakaway design. Larger signs may need more than one post and/or larger diameter posts (6"x 6", 8" x 8", 10" x 10", etc.) to provide adequate support against wind loading. Additional information on determining the number of posts needed for a sign can be found on page 3-21.

Signs should be mounted using a vandal-resistant hardware set with a 5/16"x 6"or 8" bolt for 4"x 4" and 4"x 6", respectively. If predrilled holes are desired, this should be specified on the order form. Signs intended for viewing from a road should be posted with the lower edge of the sign at least 5 feet above the level of the roadway. More detailed information on mounting signs can be found in the Installation/Mounting section, pages 3-6 through 3-9 in this manual.

Field stations may not make Information signs. In accordance with 18 USC 4124, most Information Signs must be ordered from UNICOR. (Alaska is exempt from this requirement due to shipping costs.) The Service Custom Sign Order Form (FWS-3-2040) should be used to order Information signs. These forms can be obtained from the Regional Sign Coordinator or they may be photocopied from page 3-14 of this manual.

Maintenance

Information Signs must be cleaned and inspected regularly. If a sign has been vandalized or otherwise damaged, the cost of repair in time and materials should be weighed against the cost of a replacement sign. Badly damaged signs should be replaced. More detailed information on the cleaning and repair of plywood-substrate signs can be found on pages 4-1 through 4-13 of this manual.

General Information Signs

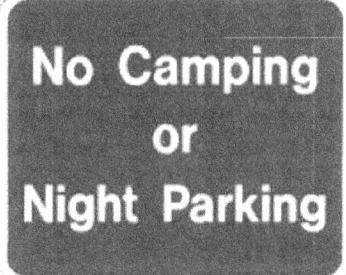

Description

General Information Signs are made of HDO plywood and have white reflective lettering and borders on a brown reflective background. If applicable, the U.S. Fee Area symbol should appear on General Information Signs. When used, this symbol should be placed to the left of the text.

Lists of permitted and prohibited activities should not be placed on the same sign. They should be on separate signs posted far enough apart to avoid confusion. Where such signs are posted along roads, they should be at least 100 feet apart.

Use/Purpose

General Information Signs inform visitors of opportunities, services, and regulations at a field station.

Concession Area Signs

Use/Purpose

Concession Area Signs identify a concession operation and provide information on rates or fees for commercial goods or services offered.

The standard substrate for Concession Area Signs is 3/4" HDO plywood with white reflective text and borders on a brown reflective background. If there is need for a title or header, it appears in the top part (1/3) of the sign and has a reverse color scheme-brown reflective letters on a white reflective background. The bottom part of the sign is brown reflective sheeting with white letters specifying service(s) and rates.

The text on Concession Area Signs, in addition to the general guidelines offered, should answer in advance visitors' likely questions by providing all essential information on rates, fees, hours, restrictions, and so on. If the information is too lengthy or complicated for a sign, it can be provided in the form of a brochure which would be made available at the sign or nearby.

Service, YCC, And Job Corps Building Designation Signs

Use/Purpose

Building Designation Signs identify station buildings and, if appropriate, show their hours of operation.

Building Designation Signs come in standard and non-standard varieties. Standard Building Designation Signs are made of 3/4" HDO plywood and have white reflective lettering and borders on a brown reflective background. The letter style is Helvetica medium. Non-standard Building Designation Signs are designed to be appropriate for the architectural style of the building and are made of the same or a complementary material.

Sleigh Ride
Tickets

Adults $5.00
Children 6-12   2.50
Under 6   Free

Visitor Center

They may be designed and made by the builder at the time the building is constructed, or they may be purchased from a commercial source. If advice regarding Building Designation Signs is needed, the Regional sign coordinator should be contacted.

Design Standards

Building Designation Signs identify buildings by name (Visitor Center, Office, etc.). If appropriate, the hours of operation should be listed, either as a permanent part of the sign, if hours remain the same all year, or on removable panels, if hours change. The Service Emblem may be used on Building Designation Signs. If the Service Emblem is used, it should appear on the left side of the sign, with all text placed to the right, using a flush left margin. Standard Building Designation Signs use Helvetica medium lettering, using both upper and lower-case letters. Removable panels should not affect sign design.

Placement

Building Designation Signs should be placed at eye level (about 5'5") on the front exterior wall of the building, near the main entrance. However, they may be placed along the building's approach road or walk at any height deemed suitable for the type of viewing they will have. Signs placed along roads must meet the same standards of design, placement, and mounting as General Information Signs (page 5-29).

Mounting

Building Designation Signs mounted on buildings should be installed with rustproof hardware suitable for the type of material from which the building is made. Others should be mounted on CCA-treated wood posts using vandal-resistant hardware.

Field stations may not make Building Designation Signs. Standard Building Designation Signs can be ordered from UNICOR using the Service Custom Sign Order Form (FWS-3-2040), plus, as appropriate, a Purchase Order, an Acquisition Request, and/or a Request for Price Quotation. The Custom Sign Order forms can be obtained from the Regional Sign Coordinator or photocopied from page 3-14 of this manual.

Non-standard Building Designation Signs may be ordered through local or other appropriate sources. Information for ordering non-standard signs is available from the Regional Sign Coordinator.

Ready Reference Guide to Guide Signs

	General Guide Signs	Advance Notice Signs
Use	Placed on Service lands to indicate: Destination distance Direction Route of travel	Place off Service lands to direct visitors to destinations on Service lands.
Description	3/4 HDO plywood substrate covered with reflectorized vinyl sheeting White reflective letters on brown reflective background	Standards are usually determined by the agency with jurisdiction over the road.
Design Standards	Sign size and letter height are determined by speed of traffic and viewing distance. Letter style is Helvetica medium. Messages always involve destination/direction information. U.S. Fee Area symbol should be used, if applicable.	Messages always direct visitors to destinations on Service lands. U.S. Fee Area symbol should be used, if applicable. Color and letter style are usually determined by the agency with jurisdiction over the road.
Placement	Signs should not be placed where they will create distractions, obstructions, or hazards. Place far enough ahead of turns for drivers to read and react safely. Signs posted along roads should generally be at least 12' from the edge of the travelled way. MUTCD guidelines should be followed when posting these signs.	
Mounting and Installation	Bottom edges of signs should be mounted 5' above the level of the road. Most guide signs can be mounted on standard 4" x 4" or 4" x 6" posts. If larger-than-standard posts are used, they must be of breakaway design unless the sign is protected by guardrail or topographic change. Mount using vandal-resistant hardware.	
Ordering	Order from UNICOR, using Service Custom Order form (FWS-3-2040).	
Maintenance	Inspect and clean regularly. Wash with a mild, biodegradable detergent and water solution. If a sign is vandalized or otherwise damaged, weight the cost of repair in time and materials against the cost of a replacement sign. Replace badly damaged signs.	

Guide Signs

Functions and Types of Guide Signs

Guide signs indicate destination, direction, and/or route of travel. This section is divided into two parts:

- General Guide signs

- Advance Notice signs

Description

General Guide signs are made of 3/4" HDO plywood and have white reflective lettering and borders on a brown reflective background. Since Advance Notice signs are usually located on state, county, or local road right-of-ways, those agencies may define suitable sign substrates, colors, and letter styles based on their standards.

General Guide Signs

Use/Purpose

General Guide Signs are signs placed on Service lands to indicate destination direction, destination distance, and/or route of travel. On Service lands, there are two main kinds of General Guide Signs: those placed along roadways for motorists and those placed along foot, bicycle, horse, and canoe trails. If a General Guide Sign is used to lead visitors to a fee area or pay booth, the U.S. Fee Area symbol should be used. Additional information on use of the U.S. Fee Area symbol can be found on pages 5-43 and 5-44.

Advance Notice Signs

Use/Purpose

Advance Notice Signs are placed off Service lands to direct visitors to destinations on Service lands. Advance Notice Signs are most helpful to visitors when they include information about limitations on visiting hours or seasons and fees, if applicable. See U.S. Fee Area symbol information on pages 5-43 through 5-44.

The use of Advance Notice Signs may require the permission/cooperation of the state, county, or other agency having jurisdiction over the approach roads or highways. Regions are encouraged to enter into Memoranda of Agreement with state or local highway agencies negotiating the terms of construction, installation, maintenance, and access regarding Advance Notice Signs.

Visitor Center 2

Design Standards

The text on General Guide Signs and Advance Notice Signs is arranged in messages. These messages always involve destination/direction information. The following guidelines should be used in developing them:

- Keep wording and messages to a minimum so it will be legible at a glance during the short time a driver can look away from the road.

- Show destinations in the following sequence:

  - Straight-ahead arrows, lowest mileage first.

- Left-turn arrows, lowest mileage first.

- Right-turn arrows, lowest mileage first.

- Place straight-ahead arrows and left-turn arrows at the left margin.

- Place right-turn arrows at the right margin.

- Indicate mileage with numbers only.

- Express parts of miles as fractions, not decimals, rounded to the nearest quarter mile.

- Use the abbreviation "ft" to indicate number of feet, and "yds" to indicate number of yards.

- Use no more than four principal messages per sign.

Generally, illustrative graphics other than Federal Recreation Symbols should not be used. However, simple theme graphics denoting established tour routes or other special features may be used sparingly and in good taste.

Sign size varies according to the size of the letters and the amount of text. Signs intended for pedestrian viewing use smaller lettering and are generally smaller in overall size. If the sign is to be read from moving vehicles, letter size is determined by traffic speed on the road where the sign is posted. Helvetica medium is the letter style, and both upper and lower-case letters are used.

Usually, the overall size of a sign is determined by the manufacturer unless there is a particular reason for the station to determine it. For instance, if there is minimum space for the sign or if the sign is to be subordinate to another sign, the station may request a certain size sign. The table on page 2-12 illustrates how to determine letter size; and once the letter size and amount of text are known, the sign size can be calculated using the chart on page 2-12.

Placement

General Guide Signs and Advance Notice Signs should be placed only where they are needed, and overuse should be avoided. Further placement guidelines include:

- Signs should not be placed where they might create distractions, obstructions, or hazards.

- Signs meant for pedestrian viewing should be placed at an appropriate level.

- Larger signs posted for viewing at greater distances can be placed proportionately higher.

- Signs posted along roads should be at least 12 feet from the edge of the traveled way.

General Guide Signs should be mounted on standard 4"x 4" or 4" x 6" CCA-treated wood posts. Use of standard posts eliminates the need for breakaway design. Larger signs may need more than one post or larger posts. Additional information on determining the number of posts needed for a sign can be found on page 3-21.

General Guide Signs should be mounted using a vandal resistant hardware set with a 5/16" x 6" or 5/16" x 8" bolt, depending on post size. If predrilled holes are desired, this should be specified on the order form. Signs intended for viewing from a road should be posted with the lower edge of the sign 5 feet above the level of the roadway. More detailed information on mounting signs can be found in the installation and mounting section, pages 3-6 through 3-9, in this manual.

Field stations may not make General Guide Signs. In accordance with 18 USC 4124, these signs must be ordered from UNICOR.

Field stations may not make General Guide Signs. In accordance with 18 USC 4124, these signs must be ordered from UNICOR.

Ordering

The Service Custom Sign Order Form (FWS-3-2040) should be used to order all General Guide Signs.

Maintenance

General Guide Signs must be cleaned and inspected regularly. If a sign has been vandalized or otherwise damaged, the cost of repair in time and materials should be weighed against the cost of a replacement sign. Badly damaged signs should be replaced. More detailed information on the cleaning and repair of plywood-substrate signs can be found on pages 4-1 through 4-13 of this manual.

INTERPRETIVE SIGNS

Functions and Types of Interpretive Signs

Interpretive Signs provide educational information related to a field station's key resources and issues. They should anticipate visitors' most basic questions. Interpretive Signs may include:

- Interior exhibits

- Trail markers

- Exterior exhibits/orientation panel

Interpretive Signs are different from all other types of signs in the following ways:

- Interpretive Signs are almost always unique, relating to the geography, geology, plant life, animal life, or historic architecture of an area. They generally have no standard messages. Instead, messages are developed to interpret specific sites, issues, or concepts.

- Interpretive Signs have a different scope and purpose than other types of signs. They are intended to be educational; thus, their messages may be longer and more complicated than those on other signs.

- Interpretive Signs can be made of any appropriate material and can be any appropriate shape or color.

Since Interpretive Signs are never intended for viewing from a moving vehicle, they are not subject to MUTCD standards of design or placement, except that they must not be placed so as to create a distraction or hazard for motorists. However, they are sometimes located at pullouts or other areas within 30 feet of a roadway. In these instances, they must meet MUTCD guidelines for breakaway supports unless they are protected by guard rail or topographic change. More information on MUTCD guidelines for breakaway sign supports can be found on page 3-22 of this manual.

The process of planning, design, and approval for Interpretive Signs is covered in the Public Use Requirements policy and guidelines, available through Regional offices. Design proposals for field exhibits and signs are approved by Regional interpretive planners and by line supervisors.

In addition, Interpretive signs are usually fabricated by private contractors instead of by UNICOR. The Winona Sign Shop can fabricate some Interpretive signs on a limited number of materials.

The Regional interpretive planner or landscape architect should be contacted for assistance on Interpretive Sign conceptualization, planning, design, and contracting.

Ordering

Field stations may not make Interpretive Signs. They may be ordered from the Winona Sign Shop using the Service Custom Sign Order Form (FWS-3-2040) and an acquisition request, or they may be contracted for through commercial sources. All proposed Interpretive Signs must be approved by the Regional line supervisor for the field station and by the Regional interpretive planner. Interpretive Signs may also be referred to other appropriate staff, such as outdoor recreation or planning specialists and Regional sign coordinator, for review.

The Service Custom Sign Order Form can be obtained from the Regional Sign Coordinator or photocopied from page 3-14 of this manual.

- Routed/Sandblasted Wood — For office display or other interior display and in appropriate outside locations. (Presently available only from private contractors).

- Porcelain on enameled steel on entrance signs.

Vehicle Mounting

The 8" Service Emblem should be placed 2 inches below the For Official Use Only-U.S. Government decal. The bottom edge of the latter should be 4 inches below the vehicle window [see 23 AM 8.61(2) and AM 9.4B(4)]. Additional information on this decal is found on page 2-5.

If the vehicle door design does not permit application in this format, the Emblem should be centered on the door with the legend centered 2 inches above it.

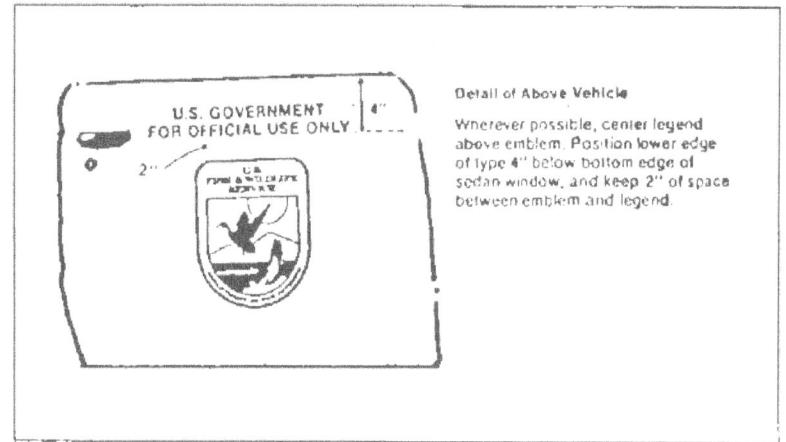

Mounting Reflective Decals

Before new decals can be applied, old decals must be completely removed and the surface cleaned. There are several ways to remove old decals:

- Heat lamp — Soften the old decal by placing a heat lamp about 18 inches away from it for about 20 minutes. After the decal is softened, peel it off with a stiff putty knife, being careful not to scratch the painted surface to which the old decal was attached.

- Steam cleaner — This method is fast and efficient. Steam cleaning services can usually be contracted locally.

- Stripping agents such as xylol, lacquer thinner or Varnish Makers and Painters naphtha. **Extreme caution** should be used with all of these agents since they can cause paint damage, are highly flammable, and can be harmful if they come into contact with skin or eyes.

Preparing the Surface — The surface to which the decal is to be applied must be clean. Remove oil, grease, and dirt using mineral spirits, and then wipe the surface dry with a clean cloth.

Applying the Decal — The reflective sheeting is designed for application at temperatures between 50 and 90 degrees F. The adhesive will not adhere well to a colder or hotter surface.

When the application surface has been cleaned, align the decal, remove the backing sheet, and gently position the decal on the surface. Tack the decal in place with finger pressure at two points on the upper edge. Once the decal is in position, press it firmly to the surface with a squeegee, starting at center and working out to edges, using overlapping strokes.

Use firm pressure with the squeegee to avoid forming air pockets near the upper corners. Lift these corners back beyond the points at which the decal was tacked to the surface. This prevents wrinkles and bubbles at the tack points.

Re-squeegee the edges using firm pressure. Finally, wipe the face of the decal with a soft cloth to remove any surface dust.

Decal Storage — Decals should be stored flat in a cool, dry place with slip sheets between them so they will not stick together under stack pressure. The normal shelf life for emblems, vehicle door legends, and other decals is about one year. After that time the protective backing begins to pull away from the edges of the decal, exposing the adhesive to air. This causes the adhesive to dry out and lessens its holding power.

Ordering
See Appendix 3 for ordering information.

Service Emblem decals and other decals must be ordered from UNICOR. Sizeable savings can be made by placing large quantity orders. Emblems and decals should be ordered by code number on standard Purchase Order (3-2103) forms. Order codes for the various decal sizes and substrates are shown in the table below. The order code incorporates the following information: FWS = Service identity; I = Information; D = Decal; R = Reflectorized; AM = substrate (aluminum or magnetic); numbers = size.

Maintenance
To clean routed emblems or mounted decals, dust the surface and wash with a damp sponge or mild soap and water solution. When cleaning decals, be careful not to loosen the edges. Cracked or damaged decals should be replaced.

Other Decals

Use/Purpose

Along with the Service Emblem decal, other decals are used to identify the Service or Service objectives by placement on official vehicles such as boats, cars, and equipment operating at field stations or on articles such as notebooks, hardhats, or large exhibits.

Description

The Service currently uses the following decals in addition to the Service Emblem decal. (See the preceding section for information on the Service Emblem decal):

- **For Official Use Only — U.S. Government vehicle door legend** Available with brown (for use on light-colored vehicles) or white (for use on dark-colored vehicles) letters on transparent background. (2"H x 10"W).

FOR OFFICIAL USE ONLY
U.S. GOVERNMENT

- **Buckle Up vehicle dash safety decal** Black letters on white background. (2 3/4"H x 4 1/2"W).

- **Youth Conservation Corps decal**
  Blue and green on white. (3" diameter).

- **U.S. Fee Area symbol**
  Blue, gold, and white. (Available in 9" and 18" diameters)

Placement

- **For Official Use Only — U.S. Government** must appear on all Service vehicles except law enforcement vehicles and those at Job Corps Civilian Conservation Centers, which have their own official-use decals (see below).

- **Buckle Up** — must be placed on the driver's side of the dashboard of all Service vehicles.

- **Job Corps For Official Use Only** — must be used on all Job Corps vehicles: the silk-screened decal should be placed on all large, heavy equipment, on the door, if possible. If not, mount neatly and conspicuously where it will not create a safety hazard. The reverse screen print decal should be placed centered at the bottom of the rear window of all other vehicles.

- The Job Corps decal may be placed on notebooks and hardhats only.

- The Youth Conservation Corps decal may be placed on notebooks and hardhats only.

- U.S. Fee Area symbol is to be posted at all public access points to entrance and user fee sites. It is available in two sizes:

  - The 9" size is designated for areas accessible by foot.
  - The 18" size is designated for use at the entrances of all fee areas and other appropriate sites where viewed from a vehicle.

When the U.S. Fee Area symbol is used on Advance Notice, Information, or Guide signs, the symbol should be placed, vertically centered, to the left of the text.

FEDERAL RECREATIONAL SYMBOLS

Use/Purpose

Federal Recreation Symbols graphically inform visitors of available services and of permitted and prohibited activities on Service lands. They may be used alone, on Guide signs, and on Information signs.

Description

- **Color** — The symbols are reflective white on a brown reflective background, except for the handicapped symbol (FWS-RS-028), which is white on blue. The slash used to denote a prohibited activity is red. The secondary legend, if any, uses brown reflective letters on a white background (except the handicapped symbol).

- **Size** — Federal Recreation Symbols are available in the following sizes:

Without Legend	With Legend
- 6" x 6"	- 6" X 8.5" (one line)
- 8" x 8"	- 8" x 10.5" (one line)
- 12" x 12"	- 12" x 16" (one line)
- 18" x 18"	- 12" x 18.5" (two lines)
- 24" x 24"	- 18" x 24" (one line)
	- 18" x 28.5" (two lines)
	- 18" x 28.5" (one line)
	- 24" x 28.5" (one line)
	- 24" x 32" (two lines)
	- 24" x 36" (three lines)

- **Substrate** — HDO 3/4" plywood covered with reflective sheeting

- **Message** — Because of widespread public recognition and acceptance of Federal Recreation Symbols, Service use of the symbols will not be accompanied by a message, with two exceptions:

-- If a symbol is new, or its use in a particular area is new, it may be accompanied by a message to help ensure understanding and compliance.

— Prohibitions will always be accompanied by an explanatory message to reinforce the impact of the sign and clarify its meaning for enforcement purposes. When an accompanying message is used, the message is put on one, two or three lines.

• **Layout** — Illustrations of typical Federal Recreation Symbol signs using messages and arrows are also available in the listing of signs available through Unicor in Appendix 2. Permitted and prohibited activities should be listed on separate signs. Slashes are always from left to right.

Placement

Federal Recreation Symbol signs may be placed where necessary to inform visitors of available services and permitted/prohibited recreational activities. Permitted and prohibited activities signs should generally be separated and placed far enough apart to avoid confusion. When posted along a road, it is recommended that they be at least 100 feet apart.

Federal Recreation Symbol signs should be mounted on 4"x 4" CCA-treated wood posts; galvanized metal posts are an acceptable alternative. Use of standard posts eliminates the need for breakaway design. Replacement signs may be mounted on existing metal posts that are in good condition. Vandal resistant hardware should be used to install the signs.

Where Federal Recreation Symbol signs are posted along a road with a speed limit of 30 mph or more, they should be:

- posted at least 12 feet from the edge of the traveled way

- mounted on the post so the lower edge of the sign is 5 feet from the level of the road

Field stations may not make Federal Recreation Symbol signs. In accordance with 18 USC 4124, these signs must be ordered from UNICOR except where they are a part of a sign made by another approved sign maker.

Maintenance

Federal Recreation Symbol signs must be cleaned and inspected regularly to ensure proper maintenance. Information on the inspection and maintenance of signs is found on pages 3-10 and 4-1, respectively, of this manual.

Ordering

The Unicor Sign and Decal list found in Appendix 2 includes a complete listing of the Federal Recreation Symbols that are available.

Standard Federal Recreation Symbol signs should be ordered by their code number, on a Purchase Order (3-2103). This form should be submitted to the Regional sign coordinator for approval. Regional sign coordinators may, at their discretion, waive the requirement for Regional approval and authorize field station managers to submit purchase orders for Federal Recreation Symbol signs directly to UNICOR.

If secondary custom legends are requested that require incorporation of arrows, mileage information, etc., the signs should be ordered by submitting the Service Custom Sign Order (FWS-3-2040) along with an Acquisition Request, showing an illustration/sketch of the sign needed.

TRAFFIC CONTROL DEVICES

Functions and Types of Traffic Control Devices

Traffic Control devices are all signs, signals, markings, and devices placed on, over, or adjacent to a road to regulate, warn, or guide traffic. This means that, in addition to the standard traffic signs, any sign posted for reading from a road that is open to public use is considered a Traffic Control sign. The Service signs that are most often placed along roads are Entrance, Information, Guide, and Federal Recreation Symbol signs. These signs are reflective and conform to federal laws regulating the design of Traffic Control signs. Area Management, Safety, and Interpretive Signs are not intended for reading from a moving vehicle and do not have to meet federal standards for Traffic Control Signs. This section is intended to clarify the use of Traffic Control Signs and devices on Service facilities and to help managers apply Traffic Control techniques to ensure safe, efficient travel on Service roads.

The *Manual on Uniform Traffic Control Devices* (MUTCD) is the official standard for use on all roads open to public travel. This means that guidelines set forth in the MUTCD govern the selection, design, and placement of all Traffic Control devices and signs posted for viewing from Service roads that are open to public travel, even if only on a seasonal or intermittent basis.

General Principles

To be effective, a sign must:

- Be necessary.
- Command attention and respect.
- Convey a clear message.
- Give adequate time for proper response.

Signs should be used only where warranted. Overuse is as bad as under use or misuse. Signs are essential where special regulations apply at specific places or at specific times and where hazards are not obvious. The standards and provisions set forth here are not intended to substitute for engineering judgment in the selection of Traffic Control devices. State or local highway departments may be consulted for assistance if needed.

The Service sign program most often uses the following types of standard Traffic Control Signs:

- **Regulatory Signs** — Regulatory signs give notice of traffic laws or regulations and include the following types of signs: stop, yield, speed, movement, turning, alignment, exclusion, one-way, parking, and pedestrian. Details on Regulatory signs are found in Part 2B of the MUTCD.

- **Warning Signs** — Warning signs call attention to conditions that are potentially hazardous on or near the road. Typical locations or hazards warranting the use of Warning signs include:

  — Changes in the horizontal alignment of the road

  — Intersections

  — Advance warning of control devices

  — Converging traffic lanes

  — Narrow roads

  — Changes in highway design

  — Grades

  — Road surface

  — Railroad or other crossings

Details on Warning signs can be found in Part 3C of the MUTCD. A listing of traffic control signs is included in the UNICOR sign and decal catalog found in Appendix 2.

As mentioned above, Service Entrance, Information, Guide, and Federal Recreation Symbol Signs are also considered to be traffic control signs for the purpose of this discussion.

Other Traffic Control Devices

The MUTCD guidelines for Traffic Control other than signs also apply on Service lands to the devices listed below. For more detailed information, consult Section III of the MUTCD.

- Road Markings

- Road Delineators

- Object Markers

- Barricades

- Road Closures

- Miscellaneous

  - Civil Defense signs

  - Traffic control for road construction and maintenance

  - Traffic control for railroad crossings

  - Traffic control for bicycle facilities

Ordering

See Appendix 2 for ordering information.

Field stations may not make Traffic Control signs or devices. In accordance with 18 USC 4124, they must be ordered from UNICOR. Traffic Control signs/devices can be ordered through the Regional sign coordinator by using their identifying code numbers on standard Purchase Order forms (3-2103). Regional Sign Coordinators may, at their discretion, waive the requirement for Regional approval of the FWS-3-2103 form and authorize field station managers to order Traffic Control Signs/devices by issuing the purchase order directly to UNICOR.

The Traffic Control signs that are most often ordered by the Service are shown in Appendix 2. Other Traffic Control signs can be found in the *Standard Highway Handbook*, dated 1979, and Revision 2, dated 1979, and/or the MUTCD.

The MUTCD sign catalog will be periodically revised by the Federal Highway Administration. Revisions will be sent directly to field stations maintaining MUTCD subscriptions with the Government Printing Office (GPO). When MUTCD revisions are received, they should be inserted into the MUTCD Manual.

SAFETY SIGNS

DANGER

NO TRESPASSING

Functions and Types of Safety Signs

Safety signs provide visitors and Service employees with information and/or rules relating to health and safety. The Safety sign system was developed in compliance with standards set by the American National Standards Institute and the Occupational Health and Safety Administration and is intended for use in both public and restricted areas of Service facilities. Following are the basic types of safety signs:

- Safety Instruction signs
- Caution signs
- Danger signs
- Hazard signs
- Notice signs
- Safety Equipment/Directions signs

The following information applies to all Safety signs:

Description

Safety signs can be made of aluminum, wood, fiberglass, or plastic, and they are also available in self-adhesive decals. Graphics, symbols, colors, and headings are standard with no options. Safety signs that bear messages have standard lists of messages available, and other messages should be used only when absolutely necessary. The messages are simple and direct with a positive tone. They are available in several sizes.

Placement

Safety signs are meant to be read by pedestrians. They are not road signs. They should be conspicuously placed in the area where they are needed without creating a distraction or a hazard in themselves.

Small signs intended for close viewing should be placed at eye level - about 5'5". Larger signs may be posted proportionately higher. Placing too many signs in one location should be avoided because it creates confusion and reduces the signs' effectiveness.

Except when absolutely necessary to fulfill their purpose, Safety signs should not be placed on or next to moveable objects (such as doors, racks, and windows) that when moved could hide the sign.

Mounting

Safety signs can be mounted on walls, fences, posts, or where necessary for maximum visibility. Fiberglass, plastic, aluminum, and poster signs can be mounted with small screws or with double-sided foam tape. The signs can be ordered with holes predrilled for mounting with screws. Predrilled holes are 1/8" in diameter, one in each of the four corners.

Ordering

See Appendix 2 for ordering information.

Field stations may not make Safety signs. In accordance with 18 USC 4124, these signs must be ordered from UNICOR.

Safety signs should be ordered by code number on standard Purchase Order (3-2103) forms. The applicable message should be selected from the lists on the following pages and spelled out on the order form. The order should be submitted to the Regional Sign Coordinator for approval and processing. Regional Sign Coordinators may, at their discretion, waive the requirement for Regional approval and authorize field station managers to submit purchase orders for safety signs directly to UNICOR. Under emergency circumstances, safety signs may be purchased by the most expedient method.

Maintenance

Safety signs are subject to Service standards of inspection and maintenance. These standards require regular inspection to ensure that the signs remain appropriate, clean, and in good condition.

Most Safety signs can be cleaned with a mild soap and water solution. The maintenance section of this manual includes instructions for repairing damaged or vandalized wood and aluminum signs, although this should be done only if it is determined that repair is more cost effective than replacing the sign. Fiberglass and plastic signs and decals should be replaced when cracked, broken, or damaged.

Sign Chapter of theAdministrative Manual — 3 AM 5 (Draft)

Table of Contents

SIGNS

5.1 Purpose. This chapter describes general policies, procedures, and responsibilities for a uniform nationwide system of standard Service signs. More specific policies, procedures, and specifications are contained in the Service Sign Manual.

5.2 Scope. The provisions of this chapter apply to all managers of Service facilities and programs. These provisions impact public awareness, public use of Service facilities, and employee and public safety.

5.3 Objectives. The objectives of this chapter are to (1) designate the Service Sign Manual as the source of Service sign policy, and (2) identify roles and responsibilities of the Service Sign Committee and facility managers regarding the proper use and placement of appropriate Service signs. Effective management of this program will promote the safety and convenience of the visiting public and employees, define boundaries, identify management practices, provide information, and protect Service resources.

5.4 Authorities. The following regulations are provided for use in the procurement, installation, maintenance, uniformity, inventory and monitoring of Service signs:

A. Title 23, U.S. Code, Sections 109(b), 109(d) and 402(a).

B. 23 CFR 1204.4 and 1230.4, and 43 CFR 8000 in its entirety.

C. National Trails Systems Act, PL 90-543.

D. Manual on Uniform Traffic Control Devices (MUTCD), Department of Transportation, Federal Highway Administration, 1978 Edition; Revision No. 1, dated December 1979; Revision No. 2, dated December 1983;

Revision No. 3, dated September, 1984; Revision No. 4, dated March 1986; and all subsequent revisions.

E. Traffic Control Devices Handbook, Department of Transportation, Federal Highway Administration, 1983.

F. Standard Highway Signs, Department of Transportation, Federal Highway Administration, 1979.

G. Highway Safety Act, PL 89-5641, dated September 9, 1966.

H. Title 18, United States Code, Section 4124.

5.5 Roles and Responsibilities. Effective management of the Service sign program requires commitment to the roles and responsibilities described below:

A. Sign Committee Chairperson. The Director designates a chairperson and appoints other members to the committee. The chairperson, as the speaker for the committee, will keep the Directorate informed of the committee's activities.

B. Sign Committee Coordinator. The coordinator, designated by the Director, is responsible for the overall coordination of the sign program, and will receive comments, criticisms, and suggestions from the committee members. The coordinator is responsible for disseminating current sign information to committee members, and will advise the chairperson on matters relating to the program. The coordinator will be the liaison officer between the Service, Federal Highway Administration, and the suppliers.

The coordinator will resolve problems encountered by regions and field stations in dealing with suppliers, schedule meetings as appropriate, develop specifications, develop sign ordering and monitoring techniques, and revise manual instructions to ensure development of a cost effective program that meets applicable legislation.

C. **Regional Coordinators.** Regional coordinators: (1) represent the Region on issues concerning signs, (2) process and approve all appropriate sign requests, (3) act as the contacts for all UNICOR orders placed in their individual Regions, (4) review requests for waivers from ordering policies and procedures and forward recommendations to the committee, (5) ensure that all stations are informed of current sign policies and procedures, (6) receive and review comments and complaints regarding the program, (7) coordinate Service testing programs and/or consolidated order requests, and (8) evaluate and monitor overall Regional compliance with Service policies and procedures.

D. **Service Sign Committee.** This is a standing committee consisting of the following representatives: (1) chairperson (typically, the Deputy Assistant Director, Refuges and Wildlife), (2) national coordinator, (3) regional coordinators (not fewer than seven members), (4) one refuge manager and one fishery resource representative, (5) a safety advisor, and (6) any other advisor(s) selected by the Director. Composition of the committee should reflect the Service organization.

Voting members of the committee are the seven regional coordinators and the refuge manager and fishery resource representative. The committee chairperson will vote in the event of a tie. A majority rule will be the basis for determining the final decisions and/or recommendations made by the committee.

A quorum will consist of five voting members excluding the chairperson.

The functions of the committee are to: (1) represent field stations, (2) coordinate and manage the sign program, (3) serve as a primary advisor to the Director, (4) review requests for waivers and forward recommendations to the Director, and (5) monitor the program and formulate recommendations for changes.

> **E. Facility Managers.** Service facility managers are responsible for becoming familiar with and implementing the inventory, installation and maintenance requirements set forth in the Sign Manual, meeting the Federal Highway Standards prescribed in the Manual on Uniform Traffic Control Devices, and applicable procurement regulations. Managers who permit the use of unauthorized signs at their facility(ies) will be considered negligent in their duties and responsibilities.

5.6 Service Standards. Servicewide standards are recommended by the Service Sign Committee and approved by the Director to ensure continuity needed to meet the objectives of the sign program. These standards enhance public accessibility, improve identity of Service facilities, increase safety, and meet legislative requirements. Use of the Service Sign Manual is mandatory for all field stations and will be monitored by the Regions to ensure compliance.

Appendix 2

UNICOR Sign and Decal Products Catalog

Appendix 3

Service, Sign and Decal Price List

Sign & Decal
Price List

U.S. Fish & Wildlife
Service

Effective April 15, 2004 thru 2006
Prices Include Shipping

F & W SERVICE EMBLEMS

STOCK NO.	DESCRIPTION	PRICE
FWS-I-DR-4	4" ADHESIVE DECAL	$ 12.19
FWS-I-DR-8	8" ADHESIVE DECAL	13.71
FWS-I-DRM-8	8" MAGNETIC DECAL	20.37
FWS-I-DRA-8	8" ALUMINUM SIGN	22.68
FWS-I-DR-12	12" ADHESIVE DECAL	17.18
FWS-I-DRM-12	12" MAGNETIC DECAL	27.20
FWS-I-DRA-12	12" ALUMINUM SIGN	27.77
FWS-I-DR-16	16" ADHESIVE DECAL	20.30
FWS-I-DRM-16	16" MAGNETIC DECAL	32.60
FWS-I-DRA-16	16" ALUMINUM SIGN	35.37
FWS-I-DR-20	20" ADHESIVE DECAL	24.29
FWS-I-DRM-20	20" MAGNETIC DECAL	40.62
FWS-I-DRA-20	20" ALUMINUM SIGN	49.93

2

DECALS

STOCK NO.	DESCRIPTION	PRICE
FWS-I-DFEE-9	US FEE AREA 9" ADHESIVE	$ 24.70
FWS-I-DFEE-18	US FEE AREA 18" ADHESIVE	29.93

FOR OFFICIAL USE ONLY
U.S. GOVERNMENT

FWS-I-JC-DR-1	FOR OFFICIAL USE ONLY	14.80
FWS-I-JC-DR-2	FOR OFFICIAL USE ONLY reverse screen size 13" x 4"	14.80
FWS-I-D-1	FOR OFFICIAL USE ONLY white on transparency	13.95
FWS-I-D-2	FOR OFFICIAL USE ONLY black on transparency	13.95
FWS-I-D-3	FOR OFFICIAL USE ONLY brown on transparency	13.95
FWS-I-D-4	FOR OFFICIAL USE ONLY cream on transparency (size: 10" x 2")	13.95
FWS-I-DB-1 BUCKLE UP.	BUCKLE UP 4.5" X 2.75"	14.00
FWS-I-YCC-1	YOUTH CONSERVATION CORPS 3" circle	26.37

3

DESIGNATED AREA SIGNS

NO
HUNTING ZONE

$24.55

FWS-A-9

PHEASANT
HUNTING ONLY

$24.55

FWS-A-10

WATERFOWL
HUNTING ONLY

$24.55

FWS-A-11

SPACED
BLIND AREA

$24.55

FWS-A-12

STEEL
SHOT ZONE

$24.55

FWS-A-13

NOTE: All signs shown are 11" x 14"

5

DESIGNATED AREA SIGNS

NATIONAL WILDERNESS AREA

$24.55

FWS-A-14

NATIONAL WILD & SCENIC RIVER AREA

$25.67

FWS-A-15

NOTE:
"DESIGNATED AREA SIGNS" are 11" x 14" on .063 Aluminum with two .375" holes.

NATIONAL WILDERNESS AREA

$24.55

FWS-A-17

YOUTH CONSERVATION CORPS

$24.62

FWS-A-16

BOUNDARY SIGNS

WATERFOWL PROTECTION AREA

$24.55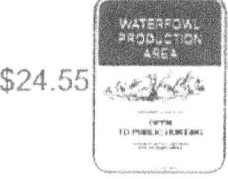

FWS-A-3

CONSERVATION EASEMENT BOUNDARY

$ 18.32 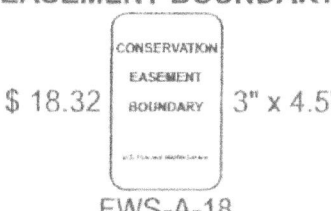 3" x 4.5"

FWS-A-18

SERVICE BOUNDARY

$24.55

FWS-A-1

REFUGE BOUNDARY

$24.55

FWS-A-2

MANAGEMENT SIGNS

100 YEAR FLOOD LEVEL

$24.55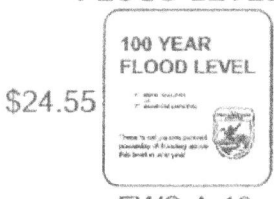

FWS-A-19

FLOOD OF RECORD

$24.55

FWS-A-20

DUCK STAMP RECOGNITION

$27.82

FWS-A-21

SEAT BELT SIGN

$27.82

FWS-A-22

www.ingramcontent.com/pod-product-compliance
Lightning Source LLC
Chambersburg PA
CBHW081214280526
45787CB00006B/2401